Work From Home

Over 300 Salaried Positions in the USA Included!

K. Swan

DEDICATION

To the ones reading this, may you find the courage, joy, and bravery contained within these pages to pursue your dreams.

CONTENTS

ACKNOWLEDGMENTS

To my amazing children, you have been my greatest source of inspiration for writing this book, which I hope will bring families closer together. I am truly grateful to you, my beloved little ones, as without your influence, this book would not have been possible. And, I must admit, I am relieved that I won't have to worry about you getting a job and living in my basement until you're 40 years old. Just kidding!

1 FORMULATING YOUR RESUME

Welcome to the bonus sections designed to assist you in your pursuit of success. Within these two sections, you will find valuable resume and interviewing tips that will prove beneficial during the initial phase of your journey towards securing a work-from-home career. It is my sincere hope that the forthcoming information will serve as a source of inspiration and instill within you the necessary confidence to persevere until you attain your desired goals. Without further ado, let us commence this endeavor!

View your resume as your personal billboard, advertising you as the ideal candidate for the job you're eyeing. Don't just list your career history; instead, curate a compelling narrative highlighting your most relevant accomplishments and skills for every job application. This technique, known as tailoring your resume, clarifies why you're the perfect fit for the role.

Always keep an updated resume blueprint handy, complete with all your qualifications. As you'll be rotating different pieces of information based on the job you're applying for, having a go-to document with previous roles, customized bullet points for various applications, and special projects becomes an invaluable tool. It's like your personal highlight reel, ready to be edited and sent out.

Prior to delving into the process of creating your own resume, it is important to acknowledge the existence of alternative options. These alternatives encompass online website builders, AI-powered resume-building platforms, and more. Nevertheless, comprehending the fundamental principles that I will be addressing will undeniably assist you in crafting a captivating resume.

It's time to bid farewell to the objective statement. The only time this relic holds any weight is when you're switching careers entirely and need to explain why your past experience doesn't align with your new path. In all other instances, an objective statement can make you seem outdated or disconnected.

Keep in mind what content is at the top of your resume. This information is what hits your eyes first when your reader looks at your resume. This eye-catching real estate is where your most pertinent qualifications should be featured on your resume. The top third of your resume is your opportunity to hook the hiring manager's attention and entice them to continue reading. If your most recent role isn't the strongest selling point, lead with a skills section or a persuasive resume summary.

Importantly, selecting the right resume format is crucial. There are numerous ways to structure your resume, like the functional resume or the combination resume. But more often than not, the trusted reverse chronological format—where your most recent experience takes the lead—is your safest bet. Unless absolutely necessary, steer clear of the functional or skills-based resume; it might raise eyebrows among hiring managers, making them wonder if you're concealing something.

There's an ongoing debate about whether a resume should span two pages or not. Here's the deal—you want your resume to be concise. Limiting it to one page helps you focus on what's truly essential. If you have a vast array of relevant experience, training, and qualifications that need more than one page, go for it. But, if you can tell your tale in a shorter space, that's even better!

There are other options, if you are struggling to fit your entire career narrative on a single page. Or, perhaps you want to showcase some examples of your work visually? Don't attempt to pack everything into your resume. Highlight the crucial details, then provide a link to your work. With your link, you can give the reader an opportunity to explore deeper into why you're the perfect fit for the role.

You might have heard rumors about computers scanning your resume to decide your employment fate. While it's not entirely accurate, many employers do use software called an Applicant Tracking System (ATS) to sift through resumes and sort them for easy access by recruiters and hiring managers. Expect your resume to encounter an ATS during your job hunt, so familiarizing yourself with its operation can streamline your search process.

I have included some tips that are ATS-friendly. Simplicity is key in your resume format. We'll touch on creativity to stand out shortly. But the golden rule of good resume formatting and design is keeping it simple. Make your resume easily digestible by using a standard font like Helvetica or Arial and leaving ample white space on the page. Your primary concern should be readability.

So, you may be asking, "How do I distinguish myself with ATS-friendly design elements?" "How do I make my resume pop among the competition?" If you're submitting your resume to an online job portal or application site, use ATS-friendly formatting elements like bold and italic text; underlining (in headings or over hyperlinks); colors; bullets; different text alignments; and columns that read straight across.

Steer clear of designs that computer systems find hard to decipher. Keep in mind that there are certain design elements that Applicant Tracking Systems (ATSs) struggle with. You would do well to avoid these: complex tables; intricate text boxes; decorative logos and icons; images and photographs; artistic graphics, graphs, or other visuals; headers and footers; exotic fonts; and columns designed to be read from top to bottom.

Let your contact information shine brightly. Though the traditional requirement of including your address on your resume is out of date, it's crucial to ensure your phone number and a professional email address are front and center. Avoid email addresses that include a hobby, food, nickname, or any other personal information. Don't forget to include other online platforms where hiring managers can find you, such as LinkedIn.

Craft your resume for speedy browsing. It's no secret that hiring managers aren't spending hours poring over each resume. Make their job easier and let them get to know you faster by designing your resume for quick and easy skimming.

There are numerous tips for portraying your work experience. Keep your work history fresh, relatively recent, and pertinent. Remember to only feature experiences that are relevant to the positions you're gunning for. And when it comes to allocating space on your resume, always prioritize importance. If you're torn between listing an internship or elaborating on your current role, opt for the latter if it is more applicable to the position you're aiming for.

It's completely normal to feel a bit anxious if you don't have any professional experience that directly aligns with the job requirements. Instead of worrying, emphasize your applicable and transferable skills in your resume, and don't forget to include any related side projects or academic achievements. To make a lasting impression, complement your resume with a compelling cover letter that tells a story of why you are the perfect fit for the job. Remember, you have valuable qualities to offer, even without prior professional experience.

Utilize bullet points to effectively communicate your strongest skills, illustrating how you have applied them and made a positive impact in your previous roles. Avoid merely listing your job responsibilities; instead, aim to provide a succinct overview of how your efforts propelled prior projects. By doing so, prospective employers will gain a clear understanding of the value you can bring to their organization.

There are some simple methods to follow while creating your bullets. Keep the number of bullets to around six. Utilize factual information, numerical data, and statistics on percentages you surpassed or individuals you helped in your bullet points to enhance their impact.

Wave goodbye to the dates in your education section once you've sailed a few years into your professional journey. When you've established yourself in your career, graduation dates begin to lose their significance. The spotlight is on whether you hold the degree, not the calendar year it was awarded. Be cautious not to unintentionally invite age discrimination, a bitter reality in certain job arenas. Additionally, enhance the impact of your resume by showcasing your commitment to lifelong learning through continuing education.

When sprucing up your resume with your skills, remember to flaunt your skills section while avoiding meaningless catchwords. Add a dedicated section that enumerates all the pertinent skills you possess for a position—especially the ones that echo the job description. I repeat, echo the job description. Avoid gaps in your resume as they can seem like red flags to employers. Highlight technical skills and include certifications and licenses that give you an edge.

To ensure perfection, it's important to meticulously proofread your work multiple times and even seek the help of others. Making a spelling mistake here would be quite bothersome. While it's usually acceptable to send your resume as a Word document, I strongly recommend using a PDF format unless instructed otherwise. Another effective way to make a lasting impression is by saving your resume as your first and last name, along with the position title and the word "resume" at the end (e.g., "ArielSmithCustomerServiceRepresentativeResume").

2 TIPS FOR A SUCCESSFUL INTERVIEW

After putting the finishing touches on your resume, it's time to dive into the interview process and take a step closer to landing your dream job. We'll cover preparation, the interview itself, and share some follow-up ideas. So, let's jump in and get started on this exciting journey!

Preparation is key for the interview. Dive headfirst into discovering the ins-and-outs of the organization and the role you're interested in. Get to know their mission, their objectives, and what they stand for. Remember, even if you've previously worked with them or for them, there's always more to learn. So, don't be complacent, keep digging!

Get familiar with your interviewer's name - know how to spell it and pronounce it. Sprinkle it throughout your interview as a sign of respect. If you're unsure, don't hesitate to call ahead and ask the secretary. And remember, the secretary's name is just as crucial, they might sway the hiring decision!

Look over your resume and application with a critical eye. Be ready to underline your past victories with solid facts and figures that align with the job's needs. Remember, every experience counts, be it paid or voluntary. Don't rest on the assumption that the interviewer knows your whole story. Gear up for game day by rehearsing your interview. Equip yourself with a solid foundation by researching common interview questions and drafting your answers.

Keep your schedule flexible and make sure you've allocated ample time for the interview. Don't forget to clarify all the nitty-gritty details - time, place, who to meet, and any other logistical aspects. Find out if you'll be facing a single interviewer or a panel. The more you know, the better prepared you can be.

Plan to beat the clock and arrive early. Consider factors such as security checks and commute time. Touch base with your point of contact to confirm the right time to arrive, check-in protocols, and other logistical details. Remember, first impressions are lasting impressions.

Be ready to deliver an elevator pitch about your experience and what you bring to the table in a concise 30-second spiel. Come prepared with your own set of queries. It's totally fine to bring a compact list of questions and ideas to the table. It demonstrates your proactive approach and eagerness to delve deeper into the organization and role.

Don't forget to pack extra copies of your resume. Keep your documents neat and orderly. Keep a trusty pen and a petite notepad handy, and avoid jotting down notes during the interview. If you feel it is necessary to jot down notes, keep it to a minimum, so it doesn't distract from the conversation. When the interview is done, make sure to record your impressions and recollections about how you think it went.

Kick off the interview with a friendly handshake and a warm smile. Eye contact is key, but remember, it's not a staring contest. Take the time to strike up a rapport. Don't rush into the thick of things. Let the interviewer set the pace. Feeling a bit jittery? That's okay! Remember, it's a learning process. With experience, you'll master the art of interviewing.

Stay focused. Highlight your strengths, your adaptable skills, and your zeal to learn. Instead of dwelling on your lack of experience, showcase how you can contribute to the organization. Honesty is the best policy. Fabrications and exaggerations are a ticking time bomb. Always stick to the truth.

Lend an attentive ear to the interviewer's every question and respond with clarity and precision. Ensure you understand the question fully. If you're unsure, don't hesitate to seek clarification or paraphrase in your own words. Be thorough yet concise in your responses and stay on topic. Highlight your accomplishments that align with the job requirements, illustrating how your expertise and skills are a perfect match.

Never badmouth a teacher, friend, employer, or your university. Keep the vibe positive and steer clear of any negative chatter about past issues. Showing loyalty is a surefire way to win over potential employers. Mind your language and tone. Be conscious of your body language and voice modulation.

Stay alert and attentive, keeping your focus on the interviewer. Articulate your thoughts accurately. Employers value candidates who can express themselves well. Even if you need to slow down or correct yourself, it's better than ungrammatical fluency.

Be ready for personal questions. Some interviewers may probe beyond the permissible limit. Plan ahead on how to tactfully handle such questions without losing your cool.

Don't hold your breath for a job offer during the first interview. You might have to sit through a couple more rounds of interviews before an offer lands on your lap a few weeks later.

Wrap up the interview on a high note. Inquire about the next steps. Show gratitude for the interviewer's time and reiterate your interest in the role. Exit the interview gracefully with a firm handshake and a genuine smile.

The interview isn't over until you've sent a thank-you note. Don't underestimate the power of expressing your gratitude for the interview and reconfirming your interest in the role, if applicable. This final step could be a game-changer. Make it count!

Remember, there are no dress rehearsals when it comes to interviews, making every moment count. Just like the spotlight on a stage, interviews place you in the limelight. Your words carry weight, and you might not get a second opportunity to impress. But here's a secret you may not be privy to - just like an actor, your performance during an interview can be heightened with well-crafted opening and closing lines. This strategy not only adds strength to your speech but also sharpens your narrative, ensuring you grab and hold your interviewers' attention. The key takeaway? Powerful opening and closing lines can strengthen your impact!

There are several strategies to consider while crafting your opening and closing lines. Start with the result of your story, then journey back to how you achieved it. Have crystal-clear messages.

Jot down the impressions you want to leave on the interviewer and brainstorm stories that highlight those qualities. Make your point unmissable. Begin with, "Let me share an example close to me...," and wrap up with, "That's the way I ..."

You can set the stage by agreeing on the importance of the topic. "We both understand the significance of ..., let me tell you how I achieved it." This serves as a testament to your understanding and assumes mutual agreement.

Initiate with phrases like: "I'm the individual who," "My colleagues would say...," "I'm renowned for ...," and "I was in charge of..." Experiment with metaphors and visual imagery to illustrate contrast, such as, "I transformed a project from A to Z." Explain your roles and achievements in the project.

Be sure to get straight to the point. "To cut a long story short, here are my strengths and what I did...," or, "Here's what transpired..." Let them imagine you on their team. Connect your opening and closing lines, so you begin and end by emphasizing the same key point.

Remember, it's not the resumes or applications that hire, it's the hiring managers. The interview is a pivotal point in the selection process, offering you a platform to elaborate on your experience, education, and training. It's also an opportunity for you to learn more about the organization and the role in question. The interview is a dialogue, with the interviewer assessing your suitability for the role, and you evaluating if the role aligns with your career aspirations. Both parties aim to gather as much information as possible to make an informed decision.

Hold your horses when it comes to salary and benefits. To get an idea of the pay scale, check out salary surveys and resources available on the Career Services website or in the career library. Please bear in mind that all discussions related to salary, perks, and other HR-related issues should be primarily directed to the HR point of contact specified in the job posting.

Patience is a virtue, especially when it comes to hiring processes. They can take a while. If you haven't heard back within the specified timeframe, feel free to check in with your point of contact.

The hiring manager is on a quest to find the perfect fit with just the right skills to fill the job opening. The stage is yours during the interview to show you are that ideal candidate. If you have any doubts, don't hesitate to reach out to your corresponding HR representative.

Now that you have crafted your resume and are ready for interviews, let's begin the process of sending out those resumes. Remember to customize each resume slightly to align with the specific position you are applying for. The job postings listed in the book are conveniently arranged in alphabetical order, with each having its own designated box to help you stay organized. While you may already be familiar with several corporations listed, it is crucial to thoroughly read the company's mission statement, purpose statement, and other relevant information. This will provide you with an advantage when tailoring your resume and preparing for interviews with them.

Don't forget that you possess the power and capability to make working from home a reality, always keep that in mind!

3 COMPANIES 1-A

1800 Contacts	Avg. $30k-$150k	https://www.1800contacts.com/careers
Yes/No	Job offered in your state and hiring?	
	What salary amount is offered?	
Yes/No	Do you like the opportunity, rate 1-5	
Yes/No	Resume/Cover letter sent/date	
Yes/No	Was the interview/Assessment Completed?	
Yes/No	Welcome Letter/Onboarding started?	
Notes:		

1800 Flowers	Avg. $30k-$130k	https://www.1800flowersinc.com/careers
Yes/No	Job offered in your state and hiring?	
	What salary amount is offered?	
Yes/No	Do you like the opportunity, rate 1-5	
Yes/No	Resume/Cover letter sent/date	
Yes/No	Was the interview/Assessment Completed?	
Yes/No	Welcome Letter/Onboarding started?	
Notes:		

AAA	Avg. $30k-$280k	https://careers.aaa.com/
Yes/No	Job offered in your state and hiring?	
	What salary amount is offered?	
Yes/No	Do you like the opportunity, rate 1-5	
Yes/No	Resume/Cover letter sent/date	
Yes/No	Was the interview/Assessment Completed?	
Yes/No	Welcome Letter/Onboarding started?	
Notes:		

ACDDIRECT.com	Avg. $70k-$108k	https://acddirect.com/careers-contractors/
Yes/No	Job offered in your state and hiring?	
	What salary amount is offered?	
Yes/No	Do you like the opportunity, rate 1-5	
Yes/No	Resume/Cover letter sent/date	
Yes/No	Was the interview/Assessment Completed?	
Yes/No	Welcome Letter/Onboarding started?	
Notes:		

Acuvue	Avg. $30k-$89k	https://www.jjvision.com/careers
Yes/No	Job offered in your state and hiring?	
	What salary amount is offered?	
Yes/No	Do you like the opportunity, rate 1-5	
Yes/No	Resume/Cover letter sent/date	
Yes/No	Was the interview/Assessment Completed?	
Yes/No	Welcome Letter/Onboarding started?	
Notes:		

Adapt Health	Avg. $30k-$287k	https://adapthealth.com/careers/
Yes/No	Job offered in your state and hiring?	
	What salary amount is offered?	
Yes/No	Do you like the opportunity, rate 1-5	
Yes/No	Resume/Cover letter sent/date	
Yes/No	Was the interview/Assessment Completed?	
Yes/No	Welcome Letter/Onboarding started?	
Notes:		

ADT	Avg. $30k-$220k	https://jobs.adt.com/
Yes/No	Job offered in your state and hiring?	
	What salary amount is offered?	
Yes/No	Do you like the opportunity, rate 1-5	
Yes/No	Resume/Cover letter sent/date	
Yes/No	Was the interview/Assessment Completed?	
Yes/No	Welcome Letter/Onboarding started?	
Notes:		

Advocate Aurora Health AAH	Avg. $20-$24hr	https://careers.aah.org/
Yes/No	Job offered in your state and hiring?	
	What salary amount is offered?	
Yes/No	Do you like the opportunity, rate 1-5	
Yes/No	Resume/Cover letter sent/date	
Yes/No	Was the interview/Assessment Completed?	
Yes/No	Welcome Letter/Onboarding started?	
Notes:		

Aetna	Avg. $37k-$297k	https://www.aetna.com/about-us.html
Yes/No	Job offered in your state and hiring?	
	What salary amount is offered?	
Yes/No	Do you like the opportunity, rate 1-5	
Yes/No	Resume/Cover letter sent/date	
Yes/No	Was the interview/Assessment Completed?	
Yes/No	Welcome Letter/Onboarding started?	
Notes:		

Afni	Avg. $14.50-$17hr	https://afnicareers.com/
Yes/No	Job offered in your state and hiring?	
	What salary amount is offered?	
Yes/No	Do you like the opportunity, rate 1-5	
Yes/No	Resume/Cover letter sent/date	
Yes/No	Was the interview/Assessment Completed?	
Yes/No	Welcome Letter/Onboarding started?	
Notes:		

A-Line Staffing	Avg. $30k-$157k	https://jobs.alinestaffing.com/
Yes/No	Job offered in your state and hiring?	
	What salary amount is offered?	
Yes/No	Do you like the opportunity, rate 1-5	
Yes/No	Resume/Cover letter sent/date	
Yes/No	Was the interview/Assessment Completed?	
Yes/No	Welcome Letter/Onboarding started?	
Notes:		

Allstate	Avg. $16-$25hr	https://careers.allstate.com/
Yes/No	Job offered in your state and hiring?	
	What salary amount is offered?	
Yes/No	Do you like the opportunity, rate 1-5	
Yes/No	Resume/Cover letter sent/date	
Yes/No	Was the interview/Assessment Completed?	
Yes/No	Welcome Letter/Onboarding started?	
Notes:		

Alluvion Staffing	Avg. $15-$25hr	https://www.alluvionhealth.org/careers/
Yes/No	Job offered in your state and hiring?	
	What salary amount is offered?	
Yes/No	Do you like the opportunity, rate 1-5	
Yes/No	Resume/Cover letter sent/date	
Yes/No	Was the interview/Assessment Completed?	
Yes/No	Welcome Letter/Onboarding started?	
Notes:		

Alma	Avg. $58k-$95k	https://almalasers.com/careers/
Yes/No	Job offered in your state and hiring?	
	What salary amount is offered?	
Yes/No	Do you like the opportunity, rate 1-5	
Yes/No	Resume/Cover letter sent/date	
Yes/No	Was the interview/Assessment Completed?	
Yes/No	Welcome Letter/Onboarding started?	
Notes:		

Alorica	Avg. $15-$25hr	https://www.alorica.com/careers/
Yes/No	Job offered in your state and hiring?	
	What salary amount is offered?	
Yes/No	Do you like the opportunity, rate 1-5	
Yes/No	Resume/Cover letter sent/date	
Yes/No	Was the interview/Assessment Completed?	
Yes/No	Welcome Letter/Onboarding started?	
Notes:		

Ambry Genetics	Avg. $20-$30hr	https://www.ambrygen.com/company/careers
Yes/No	Job offered in your state and hiring?	
	What salary amount is offered?	
Yes/No	Do you like the opportunity, rate 1-5	
Yes/No	Resume/Cover letter sent/date	
Yes/No	Was the interview/Assessment Completed?	
Yes/No	Welcome Letter/Onboarding started?	
Notes:		

American Family Ins.	Avg. $53k-$83k	https://www.amfam.com/about/careers
Yes/No	Job offered in your state and hiring?	
	What salary amount is offered?	
Yes/No	Do you like the opportunity, rate 1-5	
Yes/No	Resume/Cover letter sent/date	
Yes/No	Was the interview/Assessment Completed?	
Yes/No	Welcome Letter/Onboarding started?	
Notes:		

American Health Spec.	Avg. $30k-$131k	https://www.amerihealth.com/about-us/careers.html
Yes/No	Job offered in your state and hiring?	
	What salary amount is offered?	
Yes/No	Do you like the opportunity, rate 1-5	
Yes/No	Resume/Cover letter sent/date	
Yes/No	Was the interview/Assessment Completed?	
Yes/No	Welcome Letter/Onboarding started?	
Notes:		

American Red Cross	Avg. $16hr-$30hr	https://www.redcross.org/about-us/careers.html
Yes/No	Job offered in your state and hiring?	
	What salary amount is offered?	
Yes/No	Do you like the opportunity, rate 1-5	
Yes/No	Resume/Cover letter sent/date	
Yes/No	Was the interview/Assessment Completed?	
Yes/No	Welcome Letter/Onboarding started?	
Notes:		

AmeriHealth	Avg. $18hr-$30hr	https://www.amerihealth.com/about-us/careers.html
Yes/No	Job offered in your state and hiring?	
	What salary amount is offered?	
Yes/No	Do you like the opportunity, rate 1-5	
Yes/No	Resume/Cover letter sent/date	
Yes/No	Was the interview/Assessment Completed?	
Yes/No	Welcome Letter/Onboarding started?	
Notes:		

Amerisource Bergen	Avg. $56k-$126k	https://www.amerisourcebergen.com/careers-home
Yes/No	Job offered in your state and hiring?	
	What salary amount is offered?	
Yes/No	Do you like the opportunity, rate 1-5	
Yes/No	Resume/Cover letter sent/date	
Yes/No	Was the interview/Assessment Completed?	
Yes/No	Welcome Letter/Onboarding started?	
Notes:		

Apple	Avg. $18hr-$26hr	https://www.apple.com/careers/us/
Yes/No	Job offered in your state and hiring?	
	What salary amount is offered?	
Yes/No	Do you like the opportunity, rate 1-5	
Yes/No	Resume/Cover letter sent/date	
Yes/No	Was the interview/Assessment Completed?	
Yes/No	Welcome Letter/Onboarding started?	
Notes:		

Apria	Avg. $30k-$47k	https://careers.apria.com/
Yes/No	Job offered in your state and hiring?	
	What salary amount is offered?	
Yes/No	Do you like the opportunity, rate 1-5	
Yes/No	Resume/Cover letter sent/date	
Yes/No	Was the interview/Assessment Completed?	
Yes/No	Welcome Letter/Onboarding started?	
Notes:		

Arise	Avg. $30k-$60k	https://www.ariseworkfromhome.com/
Yes/No	Job offered in your state and hiring?	
	What salary amount is offered?	
Yes/No	Do you like the opportunity, rate 1-5	
Yes/No	Resume/Cover letter sent/date	
Yes/No	Was the interview/Assessment Completed?	
Yes/No	Welcome Letter/Onboarding started?	
Notes:		

Ascensus	Avg. $19-$22hr	https://careers.ascensus.com/home
Yes/No	Job offered in your state and hiring?	
	What salary amount is offered?	
Yes/No	Do you like the opportunity, rate 1-5	
Yes/No	Resume/Cover letter sent/date	
Yes/No	Was the interview/Assessment Completed?	
Yes/No	Welcome Letter/Onboarding started?	
Notes:		

Assurance IQ	Avg. $33k-$360k	https://careers.assurance.com/
Yes/No	Job offered in your state and hiring?	
	What salary amount is offered?	
Yes/No	Do you like the opportunity, rate 1-5	
Yes/No	Resume/Cover letter sent/date	
Yes/No	Was the interview/Assessment Completed?	
Yes/No	Welcome Letter/Onboarding started?	
Notes:		

Aston Carter	Avg. $30k-$70k	https://www.astoncarter.com/en/career-opportunities
Yes/No	Job offered in your state and hiring?	
	What salary amount is offered?	
Yes/No	Do you like the opportunity, rate 1-5	
Yes/No	Resume/Cover letter sent/date	
Yes/No	Was the interview/Assessment Completed?	
Yes/No	Welcome Letter/Onboarding started?	
Notes:		

Asurion	Avg. $19-$22hr	https://careers.asurion.com/meet-our-teams/remote-opportunities/
Yes/No	Job offered in your state and hiring?	
	What salary amount is offered?	
Yes/No	Do you like the opportunity, rate 1-5	
Yes/No	Resume/Cover letter sent/date	
Yes/No	Was the interview/Assessment Completed?	
Yes/No	Welcome Letter/Onboarding started?	
Notes:		

Axion Data Services	Avg. $34k-$70k	https://www.axiondata.com/employment/
Yes/No	Job offered in your state and hiring?	
	What salary amount is offered?	
Yes/No	Do you like the opportunity, rate 1-5	
Yes/No	Resume/Cover letter sent/date	
Yes/No	Was the interview/Assessment Completed?	
Yes/No	Welcome Letter/Onboarding started?	
Notes:		

Aya Healthcare	Avg. $29-$30hr	https://www.ayahealthcare.com/corporate-careers/jobs/
Yes/No	Job offered in your state and hiring?	
	What salary amount is offered?	
Yes/No	Do you like the opportunity, rate 1-5	
Yes/No	Resume/Cover letter sent/date	
Yes/No	Was the interview/Assessment Completed?	
Yes/No	Welcome Letter/Onboarding started?	
Notes:		

4 COMPANIES B-B

Bamboo Health	Avg. $30-$40hr	https://bamboohealth.com/careers-at-bamboo-health/
Yes/No	Job offered in your state and hiring?	
	What salary amount is offered?	
Yes/No	Do you like the opportunity, rate 1-5	
Yes/No	Resume/Cover letter sent/date	
Yes/No	Was the interview/Assessment Completed?	
Yes/No	Welcome Letter/Onboarding started?	
Notes:		

Bankers Life	Avg. $30k-$120k	https://www.bankerslife.com/careers/
Yes/No	Job offered in your state and hiring?	
	What salary amount is offered?	
Yes/No	Do you like the opportunity, rate 1-5	
Yes/No	Resume/Cover letter sent/date	
Yes/No	Was the interview/Assessment Completed?	
Yes/No	Welcome Letter/Onboarding started?	
Notes:		

BCBS	Avg. $15-$30hr	https://www.bcbs.com/about-us/careers
Yes/No	Job offered in your state and hiring?	
	What salary amount is offered?	
Yes/No	Do you like the opportunity, rate 1-5	
Yes/No	Resume/Cover letter sent/date	
Yes/No	Was the interview/Assessment Completed?	
Yes/No	Welcome Letter/Onboarding started?	
Notes:		

Beyond Finance	Avg. $37k-$120k	https://www.beyondfinance.com/careers
Yes/No	Job offered in your state and hiring?	
	What salary amount is offered?	
Yes/No	Do you like the opportunity, rate 1-5	
Yes/No	Resume/Cover letter sent/date	
Yes/No	Was the interview/Assessment Completed?	
Yes/No	Welcome Letter/Onboarding started?	
Notes:		

Bloom inst. of Technology	Avg. $25-$33hr	https://www.bloomtech.com/careers
Yes/No	Job offered in your state and hiring?	
	What salary amount is offered?	
Yes/No	Do you like the opportunity, rate 1-5	
Yes/No	Resume/Cover letter sent/date	
Yes/No	Was the interview/Assessment Completed?	
Yes/No	Welcome Letter/Onboarding started?	
Notes:		

Bloom Insurance	Avg. $50k-$120k	https://www.bloominsuranceagency.com/careers/
Yes/No	Job offered in your state and hiring?	
	What salary amount is offered?	
Yes/No	Do you like the opportunity, rate 1-5	
Yes/No	Resume/Cover letter sent/date	
Yes/No	Was the interview/Assessment Completed?	
Yes/No	Welcome Letter/Onboarding started?	
Notes:		

BlueJay MobileHealth	Avg. $38k-$120k	http://bluejayhealth.com/careers-at-bluejay-mobile-health.html
Yes/No	Job offered in your state and hiring?	
	What salary amount is offered?	
Yes/No	Do you like the opportunity, rate 1-5	
Yes/No	Resume/Cover letter sent/date	
Yes/No	Was the interview/Assessment Completed?	
Yes/No	Welcome Letter/Onboarding started?	
Notes:		

Blue Shield of California	Avg. $30k-$120k	https://www.blueshieldca.com/en/home/about-blue-shield/careers
Yes/No	Job offered in your state and hiring?	
	What salary amount is offered?	
Yes/No	Do you like the opportunity, rate 1-5	
Yes/No	Resume/Cover letter sent/date	
Yes/No	Was the interview/Assessment Completed?	
Yes/No	Welcome Letter/Onboarding started?	
Notes:		

Bodly	Avg. $24-$28hr	https://boldly.com/jobs/
Yes/No	Job offered in your state and hiring?	
	What salary amount is offered?	
Yes/No	Do you like the opportunity, rate 1-5	
Yes/No	Resume/Cover letter sent/date	
Yes/No	Was the interview/Assessment Completed?	
Yes/No	Welcome Letter/Onboarding started?	
Notes:		

Boston Medical	Avg. $30k-$130k	https://jobs.bmc.org/
Yes/No	Job offered in your state and hiring?	
	What salary amount is offered?	
Yes/No	Do you like the opportunity, rate 1-5	
Yes/No	Resume/Cover letter sent/date	
Yes/No	Was the interview/Assessment Completed?	
Yes/No	Welcome Letter/Onboarding started?	
Notes:		

Bread Financial	Avg. $18-$24hr	https://www.breadfinancial.com/en/who-we-are/careers.html
Yes/No	Job offered in your state and hiring?	
	What salary amount is offered?	
Yes/No	Do you like the opportunity, rate 1-5	
Yes/No	Resume/Cover letter sent/date	
Yes/No	Was the interview/Assessment Completed?	
Yes/No	Welcome Letter/Onboarding started?	
Notes:		

Brighton	Avg. $30k-$60k	https://www.brighton.com/pages/careers
Yes/No	Job offered in your state and hiring?	
	What salary amount is offered?	
Yes/No	Do you like the opportunity, rate 1-5	
Yes/No	Resume/Cover letter sent/date	
Yes/No	Was the interview/Assessment Completed?	
Yes/No	Welcome Letter/Onboarding started?	
Notes:		

Brightree	Avg. $21-$31hr	https://www.brightree.com/careers/
Yes/No	Job offered in your state and hiring?	
	What salary amount is offered?	
Yes/No	Do you like the opportunity, rate 1-5	
Yes/No	Resume/Cover letter sent/date	
Yes/No	Was the interview/Assessment Completed?	
Yes/No	Welcome Letter/Onboarding started?	
Notes:		

Broadpath.com	Avg. $30k-$40k	https://broad-path.com/
Yes/No	Job offered in your state and hiring?	
	What salary amount is offered?	
Yes/No	Do you like the opportunity, rate 1-5	
Yes/No	Resume/Cover letter sent/date	
Yes/No	Was the interview/Assessment Completed?	
Yes/No	Welcome Letter/Onboarding started?	
Notes:		

Burlington	Avg. $30k-$80k	https://www.burlington.com/about/careers/
Yes/No	Job offered in your state and hiring?	
	What salary amount is offered?	
Yes/No	Do you like the opportunity, rate 1-5	
Yes/No	Resume/Cover letter sent/date	
Yes/No	Was the interview/Assessment Completed?	
Yes/No	Welcome Letter/Onboarding started?	
Notes:		

5 COMPANIES C-C

Cadence	Avg. $20-$25hr	https://www.cadence.com/en_US/home/company/careers.html
Yes/No	Job offered in your state and hiring?	
	What salary amount is offered?	
Yes/No	Do you like the opportunity, rate 1-5	
Yes/No	Resume/Cover letter sent/date	
Yes/No	Was the interview/Assessment Completed?	
Yes/No	Welcome Letter/Onboarding started?	
Notes:		

Calm	Avg. $52k-$73k	https://www.calm.com/careers
Yes/No	Job offered in your state and hiring?	
	What salary amount is offered?	
Yes/No	Do you like the opportunity, rate 1-5	
Yes/No	Resume/Cover letter sent/date	
Yes/No	Was the interview/Assessment Completed?	
Yes/No	Welcome Letter/Onboarding started?	
Notes:		

Capital One	Avg. $30k-$50k	https://www.capitalonecareers.com/location/remote-jobs/
Yes/No	Job offered in your state and hiring?	
	What salary amount is offered?	
Yes/No	Do you like the opportunity, rate 1-5	
Yes/No	Resume/Cover letter sent/date	
Yes/No	Was the interview/Assessment Completed?	
Yes/No	Welcome Letter/Onboarding started?	
Notes:		

Capital Rx	Avg. $45k-$55k	https://www.cap-rx.com/about/careers
Yes/No	Job offered in your state and hiring?	
	What salary amount is offered?	
Yes/No	Do you like the opportunity, rate 1-5	
Yes/No	Resume/Cover letter sent/date	
Yes/No	Was the interview/Assessment Completed?	
Yes/No	Welcome Letter/Onboarding started?	
Notes:		

CareCentrix	Avg. $32k-$50k	https://www.carecentrix.com/about-us/careers/
Yes/No	Job offered in your state and hiring?	
	What salary amount is offered?	
Yes/No	Do you like the opportunity, rate 1-5	
Yes/No	Resume/Cover letter sent/date	
Yes/No	Was the interview/Assessment Completed?	
Yes/No	Welcome Letter/Onboarding started?	
Notes:		

CarMax	Avg. $30k-$500k	https://careers.carmax.com/us/en/
Yes/No	Job offered in your state and hiring?	
	What salary amount is offered?	
Yes/No	Do you like the opportunity, rate 1-5	
Yes/No	Resume/Cover letter sent/date	
Yes/No	Was the interview/Assessment Completed?	
Yes/No	Welcome Letter/Onboarding started?	
Notes:		

Carnival Cruise	Avg. $30k-$110k	https://jobs.carnival.com/
Yes/No	Job offered in your state and hiring?	
	What salary amount is offered?	
Yes/No	Do you like the opportunity, rate 1-5	
Yes/No	Resume/Cover letter sent/date	
Yes/No	Was the interview/Assessment Completed?	
Yes/No	Welcome Letter/Onboarding started?	
Notes:		

CatPerson	Avg. $48k-$56k	https://boards.greenhouse.io/catperson
Yes/No	Job offered in your state and hiring?	
	What salary amount is offered?	
Yes/No	Do you like the opportunity, rate 1-5	
Yes/No	Resume/Cover letter sent/date	
Yes/No	Was the interview/Assessment Completed?	
Yes/No	Welcome Letter/Onboarding started?	
Notes:		

CCC Intelligent Sol.	Avg. $35k-$50k	https://cccis.com/about/careers/
Yes/No	Job offered in your state and hiring?	
	What salary amount is offered?	
Yes/No	Do you like the opportunity, rate 1-5	
Yes/No	Resume/Cover letter sent/date	
Yes/No	Was the interview/Assessment Completed?	
Yes/No	Welcome Letter/Onboarding started?	
Notes:		

Centauri Health Sol.	Avg. $35k-$50k	https://www.centaurihs.com/careers/
Yes/No	Job offered in your state and hiring?	
	What salary amount is offered?	
Yes/No	Do you like the opportunity, rate 1-5	
Yes/No	Resume/Cover letter sent/date	
Yes/No	Was the interview/Assessment Completed?	
Yes/No	Welcome Letter/Onboarding started?	
Notes:		

Centene	Avg. $35k-$150k	https://jobs.centene.com/us/en
Yes/No	Job offered in your state and hiring?	
	What salary amount is offered?	
Yes/No	Do you like the opportunity, rate 1-5	
Yes/No	Resume/Cover letter sent/date	
Yes/No	Was the interview/Assessment Completed?	
Yes/No	Welcome Letter/Onboarding started?	
Notes:		

Chapter Member Adv.	Avg. $35k-$50k	https://indeed.com/
Yes/No	Job offered in your state and hiring?	
	What salary amount is offered?	
Yes/No	Do you like the opportunity, rate 1-5	
Yes/No	Resume/Cover letter sent/date	
Yes/No	Was the interview/Assessment Completed?	
Yes/No	Welcome Letter/Onboarding started?	
Notes:		

Chewy	Avg. $30k-$150k	https://careers.chewy.com/us/en/home
Yes/No	Job offered in your state and hiring?	
	What salary amount is offered?	
Yes/No	Do you like the opportunity, rate 1-5	
Yes/No	Resume/Cover letter sent/date	
Yes/No	Was the interview/Assessment Completed?	
Yes/No	Welcome Letter/Onboarding started?	
Notes:		

Cigna	Avg. $35k-$50k	https://jobs.thecignagroup.com/us/en/remote-jobs
Yes/No	Job offered in your state and hiring?	
	What salary amount is offered?	
Yes/No	Do you like the opportunity, rate 1-5	
Yes/No	Resume/Cover letter sent/date	
Yes/No	Was the interview/Assessment Completed?	
Yes/No	Welcome Letter/Onboarding started?	
Notes:		

CIOX Health	Avg. $30k-$150k	https://www.cioxhealth.com/about-us/people-culture/careers/
Yes/No	Job offered in your state and hiring?	
	What salary amount is offered?	
Yes/No	Do you like the opportunity, rate 1-5	
Yes/No	Resume/Cover letter sent/date	
Yes/No	Was the interview/Assessment Completed?	
Yes/No	Welcome Letter/Onboarding started?	
Notes:		

City of Hope	Avg. $35k-$50k	https://www.cityofhope.org/careers
Yes/No	Job offered in your state and hiring?	
	What salary amount is offered?	
Yes/No	Do you like the opportunity, rate 1-5	
Yes/No	Resume/Cover letter sent/date	
Yes/No	Was the interview/Assessment Completed?	
Yes/No	Welcome Letter/Onboarding started?	
Notes:		

Clarity Voice	Avg. $30k-$60k	https://clarityvoice.com/about/careers/open-positions/
Yes/No	Job offered in your state and hiring?	
	What salary amount is offered?	
Yes/No	Do you like the opportunity, rate 1-5	
Yes/No	Resume/Cover letter sent/date	
Yes/No	Was the interview/Assessment Completed?	
Yes/No	Welcome Letter/Onboarding started?	
Notes:		

Classy	Avg. $50k-$60k	https://www.classy.org/careers/
Yes/No	Job offered in your state and hiring?	
	What salary amount is offered?	
Yes/No	Do you like the opportunity, rate 1-5	
Yes/No	Resume/Cover letter sent/date	
Yes/No	Was the interview/Assessment Completed?	
Yes/No	Welcome Letter/Onboarding started?	
Notes:		

Cleveland Clinic	Avg. $30k-$200k	https://jobs.clevelandclinic.org/
Yes/No	Job offered in your state and hiring?	
	What salary amount is offered?	
Yes/No	Do you like the opportunity, rate 1-5	
Yes/No	Resume/Cover letter sent/date	
Yes/No	Was the interview/Assessment Completed?	
Yes/No	Welcome Letter/Onboarding started?	
Notes:		

Cohere Health	Avg. $35k-$60k	https://coherehealth.com/careers/
Yes/No	Job offered in your state and hiring?	
	What salary amount is offered?	
Yes/No	Do you like the opportunity, rate 1-5	
Yes/No	Resume/Cover letter sent/date	
Yes/No	Was the interview/Assessment Completed?	
Yes/No	Welcome Letter/Onboarding started?	
Notes:		

Coin Flip	Avg. $30k-$120k	https://builtin.com/company/coinflip
Yes/No	Job offered in your state and hiring?	
	What salary amount is offered?	
Yes/No	Do you like the opportunity, rate 1-5	
Yes/No	Resume/Cover letter sent/date	
Yes/No	Was the interview/Assessment Completed?	
Yes/No	Welcome Letter/Onboarding started?	
Notes:		

Comcast	Avg. $30k-$50k	https://jobs.comcast.com/
Yes/No	Job offered in your state and hiring?	
	What salary amount is offered?	
Yes/No	Do you like the opportunity, rate 1-5	
Yes/No	Resume/Cover letter sent/date	
Yes/No	Was the interview/Assessment Completed?	
Yes/No	Welcome Letter/Onboarding started?	
Notes:		

Common Wealth Financ	Avg. $40k-$120k	https://careers-commonwealth.icims.com/jobs/
Yes/No	Job offered in your state and hiring?	
	What salary amount is offered?	
Yes/No	Do you like the opportunity, rate 1-5	
Yes/No	Resume/Cover letter sent/date	
Yes/No	Was the interview/Assessment Completed?	
Yes/No	Welcome Letter/Onboarding started?	
Notes:		

Comphcs.com	Avg. $30k-$120k	https://comphcs.com/employment/
Yes/No	Job offered in your state and hiring?	
	What salary amount is offered?	
Yes/No	Do you like the opportunity, rate 1-5	
Yes/No	Resume/Cover letter sent/date	
Yes/No	Was the interview/Assessment Completed?	
Yes/No	Welcome Letter/Onboarding started?	
Notes:		

Concentrix	Avg. $30k-$40k	https://jobs.concentrix.com/global/en https://careers.concentrix.com/work-at-home/
Yes/No	Job offered in your state and hiring?	
	What salary amount is offered?	
Yes/No	Do you like the opportunity, rate 1-5	
Yes/No	Resume/Cover letter sent/date	
Yes/No	Was the interview/Assessment Completed?	
Yes/No	Welcome Letter/Onboarding started?	
Notes:		

Conduent	Avg. $30k-$50k	https://www.conduent.com/customer-experience-management/work-at-home/
Yes/No	Job offered in your state and hiring?	
	What salary amount is offered?	
Yes/No	Do you like the opportunity, rate 1-5	
Yes/No	Resume/Cover letter sent/date	
Yes/No	Was the interview/Assessment Completed?	
Yes/No	Welcome Letter/Onboarding started?	
Notes:		

Connection	Avg. $30k-$40k	https://www.connection.com/content/careers
Yes/No	Job offered in your state and hiring?	
	What salary amount is offered?	
Yes/No	Do you like the opportunity, rate 1-5	
Yes/No	Resume/Cover letter sent/date	
Yes/No	Was the interview/Assessment Completed?	
Yes/No	Welcome Letter/Onboarding started?	
Notes:		

Connexus Resource G	Avg. $30k-$80k	https://connexusresourcegroup.com/careers/
Yes/No	Job offered in your state and hiring?	
	What salary amount is offered?	
Yes/No	Do you like the opportunity, rate 1-5	
Yes/No	Resume/Cover letter sent/date	
Yes/No	Was the interview/Assessment Completed?	
Yes/No	Welcome Letter/Onboarding started?	
Notes:		

Continuum	Avg. $30k-$40k	https://careers.continuumgbl.com/
Yes/No	Job offered in your state and hiring?	
	What salary amount is offered?	
Yes/No	Do you like the opportunity, rate 1-5	
Yes/No	Resume/Cover letter sent/date	
Yes/No	Was the interview/Assessment Completed?	
Yes/No	Welcome Letter/Onboarding started?	
Notes:		

CPRE	Avg. $35k-$50k	https://www.cbre.com/careers/
Yes/No	Job offered in your state and hiring?	
	What salary amount is offered?	
Yes/No	Do you like the opportunity, rate 1-5	
Yes/No	Resume/Cover letter sent/date	
Yes/No	Was the interview/Assessment Completed?	
Yes/No	Welcome Letter/Onboarding started?	
Notes:		

CPRE	Avg. $35k-$50k	https://www.cbre.com/careers/
Yes/No	Job offered in your state and hiring?	
	What salary amount is offered?	
Yes/No	Do you like the opportunity, rate 1-5	
Yes/No	Resume/Cover letter sent/date	
Yes/No	Was the interview/Assessment Completed?	
Yes/No	Welcome Letter/Onboarding started?	
Notes:		

CPS	Avg. $30k-$140k	Search online for you local state CPS job site
Yes/No	Job offered in your state and hiring?	
	What salary amount is offered?	
Yes/No	Do you like the opportunity, rate 1-5	
Yes/No	Resume/Cover letter sent/date	
Yes/No	Was the interview/Assessment Completed?	
Yes/No	Welcome Letter/Onboarding started?	
Notes:		

Credit Acceptance	Avg. $30k-$50k	https://www.creditacceptance.com/careers
Yes/No	Job offered in your state and hiring?	
	What salary amount is offered?	
Yes/No	Do you like the opportunity, rate 1-5	
Yes/No	Resume/Cover letter sent/date	
Yes/No	Was the interview/Assessment Completed?	
Yes/No	Welcome Letter/Onboarding started?	
Notes:		

Curology	Avg. $57k-$80k	https://curology.com/careers/
Yes/No	Job offered in your state and hiring?	
	What salary amount is offered?	
Yes/No	Do you like the opportunity, rate 1-5	
Yes/No	Resume/Cover letter sent/date	
Yes/No	Was the interview/Assessment Completed?	
Yes/No	Welcome Letter/Onboarding started?	
Notes:		

CVS	Avg. $30k-$50k	https://jobs.cvshealth.com/Remote-Jobs/
Yes/No	Job offered in your state and hiring?	
	What salary amount is offered?	
Yes/No	Do you like the opportunity, rate 1-5	
Yes/No	Resume/Cover letter sent/date	
Yes/No	Was the interview/Assessment Completed?	
Yes/No	Welcome Letter/Onboarding started?	
Notes:		

6 COMPANIES D-G

Danaher Corp.	Avg. $50k-$320k	https://jobs.danaher.com/global/en
Yes/No	Job offered in your state and hiring?	
	What salary amount is offered?	
Yes/No	Do you like the opportunity, rate 1-5	
Yes/No	Resume/Cover letter sent/date	
Yes/No	Was the interview/Assessment Completed?	
Yes/No	Welcome Letter/Onboarding started?	
Notes:		

Davita	Avg. $38k-$120k	https://careers.davita.com/
Yes/No	Job offered in your state and hiring?	
	What salary amount is offered?	
Yes/No	Do you like the opportunity, rate 1-5	
Yes/No	Resume/Cover letter sent/date	
Yes/No	Was the interview/Assessment Completed?	
Yes/No	Welcome Letter/Onboarding started?	
Notes:		

Delta Airlines	Avg. $40k-$50k	https://www.delta.com/us/en/careers/overview
Yes/No	Job offered in your state and hiring?	
	What salary amount is offered?	
Yes/No	Do you like the opportunity, rate 1-5	
Yes/No	Resume/Cover letter sent/date	
Yes/No	Was the interview/Assessment Completed?	
Yes/No	Welcome Letter/Onboarding started?	
Notes:		

Delta Dental	Avg. $40k-$60k	https://www.deltadental.com/us/en/about-us/careers.html
Yes/No	Job offered in your state and hiring?	
	What salary amount is offered?	
Yes/No	Do you like the opportunity, rate 1-5	
Yes/No	Resume/Cover letter sent/date	
Yes/No	Was the interview/Assessment Completed?	
Yes/No	Welcome Letter/Onboarding started?	
Notes:		

DHL	Avg. $30k-$50k	https://careers.dhl.com/amer/en
Yes/No	Job offered in your state and hiring?	
	What salary amount is offered?	
Yes/No	Do you like the opportunity, rate 1-5	
Yes/No	Resume/Cover letter sent/date	
Yes/No	Was the interview/Assessment Completed?	
Yes/No	Welcome Letter/Onboarding started?	
Notes:		

Direct Interactions	Avg. $40k-$40k	https://directinteractions.com/careers
Yes/No	Job offered in your state and hiring?	
	What salary amount is offered?	
Yes/No	Do you like the opportunity, rate 1-5	
Yes/No	Resume/Cover letter sent/date	
Yes/No	Was the interview/Assessment Completed?	
Yes/No	Welcome Letter/Onboarding started?	
Notes:		

Discover	Avg. $40k-$60k	https://jobs.discovery.com/careers-home/jobs
Yes/No	Job offered in your state and hiring?	
	What salary amount is offered?	
Yes/No	Do you like the opportunity, rate 1-5	
Yes/No	Resume/Cover letter sent/date	
Yes/No	Was the interview/Assessment Completed?	
Yes/No	Welcome Letter/Onboarding started?	
Notes:		

DRW	Avg. $35k-$48k	https://www.dwr.com/brands-jobs
Yes/No	Job offered in your state and hiring?	
	What salary amount is offered?	
Yes/No	Do you like the opportunity, rate 1-5	
Yes/No	Resume/Cover letter sent/date	
Yes/No	Was the interview/Assessment Completed?	
Yes/No	Welcome Letter/Onboarding started?	
Notes:		

EHealth	Avg. $30k-$40k	https://www.ehealthinsurance.com/resources/careers
Yes/No	Job offered in your state and hiring?	
	What salary amount is offered?	
Yes/No	Do you like the opportunity, rate 1-5	
Yes/No	Resume/Cover letter sent/date	
Yes/No	Was the interview/Assessment Completed?	
Yes/No	Welcome Letter/Onboarding started?	
Notes:		

Elevance Health	Avg. $30k-$110k	https://careers.elevancehealth.com/careers/
Yes/No	Job offered in your state and hiring?	
	What salary amount is offered?	
Yes/No	Do you like the opportunity, rate 1-5	
Yes/No	Resume/Cover letter sent/date	
Yes/No	Was the interview/Assessment Completed?	
Yes/No	Welcome Letter/Onboarding started?	
Notes:		

Ecompass Health	Avg. $30k-$140k	https://careers.encompasshealth.com/
Yes/No	Job offered in your state and hiring?	
	What salary amount is offered?	
Yes/No	Do you like the opportunity, rate 1-5	
Yes/No	Resume/Cover letter sent/date	
Yes/No	Was the interview/Assessment Completed?	
Yes/No	Welcome Letter/Onboarding started?	
Notes:		

Enterprise Rental Car	Avg. $38k-$50k	https://careers.enterprise.com/
Yes/No	Job offered in your state and hiring?	
	What salary amount is offered?	
Yes/No	Do you like the opportunity, rate 1-5	
Yes/No	Resume/Cover letter sent/date	
Yes/No	Was the interview/Assessment Completed?	
Yes/No	Welcome Letter/Onboarding started?	
Notes:		

Everise	Avg. $38k-$40k	https://weareeverise.com/work-for-us/
Yes/No	Job offered in your state and hiring?	
	What salary amount is offered?	
Yes/No	Do you like the opportunity, rate 1-5	
Yes/No	Resume/Cover letter sent/date	
Yes/No	Was the interview/Assessment Completed?	
Yes/No	Welcome Letter/Onboarding started?	
Notes:		

Exemplis	Avg. $30k-$40k	https://www.exemplis.com/careers.html
Yes/No	Job offered in your state and hiring?	
	What salary amount is offered?	
Yes/No	Do you like the opportunity, rate 1-5	
Yes/No	Resume/Cover letter sent/date	
Yes/No	Was the interview/Assessment Completed?	
Yes/No	Welcome Letter/Onboarding started?	
Notes:		

EXP World Holdings	Avg. $38k-$50k	https://expworldholdings.com/careers/
Yes/No	Job offered in your state and hiring?	
	What salary amount is offered?	
Yes/No	Do you like the opportunity, rate 1-5	
Yes/No	Resume/Cover letter sent/date	
Yes/No	Was the interview/Assessment Completed?	
Yes/No	Welcome Letter/Onboarding started?	
Notes:		

FedEx	Avg. $38k-$50k	https://careers.fedex.com/fedex/
Yes/No	Job offered in your state and hiring?	
	What salary amount is offered?	
Yes/No	Do you like the opportunity, rate 1-5	
Yes/No	Resume/Cover letter sent/date	
Yes/No	Was the interview/Assessment Completed?	
Yes/No	Welcome Letter/Onboarding started?	
Notes:		

FEP Blue	Avg. $30k-$60k	https://indeed.com/
Yes/No	Job offered in your state and hiring?	
	What salary amount is offered?	
Yes/No	Do you like the opportunity, rate 1-5	
Yes/No	Resume/Cover letter sent/date	
Yes/No	Was the interview/Assessment Completed?	
Yes/No	Welcome Letter/Onboarding started?	
Notes:		

First Source	Avg. $38k-$150k	https://firsthire.taleo.net/
Yes/No	Job offered in your state and hiring?	
	What salary amount is offered?	
Yes/No	Do you like the opportunity, rate 1-5	
Yes/No	Resume/Cover letter sent/date	
Yes/No	Was the interview/Assessment Completed?	
Yes/No	Welcome Letter/Onboarding started?	
Notes:		

FIS Global	Avg. $38k-$150k	https://careers.fisglobal.com/us/en
Yes/No	Job offered in your state and hiring?	
	What salary amount is offered?	
Yes/No	Do you like the opportunity, rate 1-5	
Yes/No	Resume/Cover letter sent/date	
Yes/No	Was the interview/Assessment Completed?	
Yes/No	Welcome Letter/Onboarding started?	
Notes:		

Fiserv	Avg. $38k-$120k	https://www.careers.fiserv.com/
Yes/No	Job offered in your state and hiring?	
	What salary amount is offered?	
Yes/No	Do you like the opportunity, rate 1-5	
Yes/No	Resume/Cover letter sent/date	
Yes/No	Was the interview/Assessment Completed?	
Yes/No	Welcome Letter/Onboarding started?	
Notes:		

Five Below	Avg. $38k-$100k	https://www.fivebelow.com/info/careers
Yes/No	Job offered in your state and hiring?	
	What salary amount is offered?	
Yes/No	Do you like the opportunity, rate 1-5	
Yes/No	Resume/Cover letter sent/date	
Yes/No	Was the interview/Assessment Completed?	
Yes/No	Welcome Letter/Onboarding started?	
Notes:		

Frenenius Medical Care	Avg. $38k-$100k	https://jobs.fmcna.com/
Yes/No	Job offered in your state and hiring?	
	What salary amount is offered?	
Yes/No	Do you like the opportunity, rate 1-5	
Yes/No	Resume/Cover letter sent/date	
Yes/No	Was the interview/Assessment Completed?	
Yes/No	Welcome Letter/Onboarding started?	
Notes:		

Furguson	Avg. $30k-$40k	https://www.ferguson.com/content/careers
Yes/No	Job offered in your state and hiring?	
	What salary amount is offered?	
Yes/No	Do you like the opportunity, rate 1-5	
Yes/No	Resume/Cover letter sent/date	
Yes/No	Was the interview/Assessment Completed?	
Yes/No	Welcome Letter/Onboarding started?	
Notes:		

GAF	Avg. $42k-$50k	https://www.gaf.com/en-us/about-us/careers
Yes/No	Job offered in your state and hiring?	
	What salary amount is offered?	
Yes/No	Do you like the opportunity, rate 1-5	
Yes/No	Resume/Cover letter sent/date	
Yes/No	Was the interview/Assessment Completed?	
Yes/No	Welcome Letter/Onboarding started?	
Notes:		

Gametime	Avg. $40k-$50k	https://gametime.co/careers
Yes/No	Job offered in your state and hiring?	
	What salary amount is offered?	
Yes/No	Do you like the opportunity, rate 1-5	
Yes/No	Resume/Cover letter sent/date	
Yes/No	Was the interview/Assessment Completed?	
Yes/No	Welcome Letter/Onboarding started?	
Notes:		

Genpact	Avg. $32k-$50k	https://www.genpact.com/careers
Yes/No	Job offered in your state and hiring?	
	What salary amount is offered?	
Yes/No	Do you like the opportunity, rate 1-5	
Yes/No	Resume/Cover letter sent/date	
Yes/No	Was the interview/Assessment Completed?	
Yes/No	Welcome Letter/Onboarding started?	
Notes:		

Globalus 231	Avg. $80k-$120k	https://globalus231.dayforcehcm.com/CandidatePortal/en-US/acttoday
Yes/No	Job offered in your state and hiring?	
	What salary amount is offered?	
Yes/No	Do you like the opportunity, rate 1-5	
Yes/No	Resume/Cover letter sent/date	
Yes/No	Was the interview/Assessment Completed?	
Yes/No	Welcome Letter/Onboarding started?	
Notes:		

Good Leap	Avg. $50k-$90k	https://goodleap.com/careers/
Yes/No	Job offered in your state and hiring?	
	What salary amount is offered?	
Yes/No	Do you like the opportunity, rate 1-5	
Yes/No	Resume/Cover letter sent/date	
Yes/No	Was the interview/Assessment Completed?	
Yes/No	Welcome Letter/Onboarding started?	
Notes:		

Guardian Life	Avg. 40k-$50k	https://www.guardianlife.com/careers
Yes/No	Job offered in your state and hiring?	
	What salary amount is offered?	
Yes/No	Do you like the opportunity, rate 1-5	
Yes/No	Resume/Cover letter sent/date	
Yes/No	Was the interview/Assessment Completed?	
Yes/No	Welcome Letter/Onboarding started?	
Notes:		

Guild Mortgage	Avg. 32k-$120k	https://www.guildmortgage.com/careers/
Yes/No	Job offered in your state and hiring?	
	What salary amount is offered?	
Yes/No	Do you like the opportunity, rate 1-5	
Yes/No	Resume/Cover letter sent/date	
Yes/No	Was the interview/Assessment Completed?	
Yes/No	Welcome Letter/Onboarding started?	
Notes:		

Guild.com	Avg. 35k-$60k	https://www.guild.com/careers/
Yes/No	Job offered in your state and hiring?	
	What salary amount is offered?	
Yes/No	Do you like the opportunity, rate 1-5	
Yes/No	Resume/Cover letter sent/date	
Yes/No	Was the interview/Assessment Completed?	
Yes/No	Welcome Letter/Onboarding started?	
Notes:		

Gusto	Avg. 40k-$60k	https://gusto.com/about/careers
Yes/No	Job offered in your state and hiring?	
	What salary amount is offered?	
Yes/No	Do you like the opportunity, rate 1-5	
Yes/No	Resume/Cover letter sent/date	
Yes/No	Was the interview/Assessment Completed?	
Yes/No	Welcome Letter/Onboarding started?	
Notes:		

7 COMPANIES H-J

Hartford	Avg. 40k-$60k	https://www.thehartford.com/careers
Yes/No	Job offered in your state and hiring?	
	What salary amount is offered?	
Yes/No	Do you like the opportunity, rate 1-5	
Yes/No	Resume/Cover letter sent/date	
Yes/No	Was the interview/Assessment Completed?	
Yes/No	Welcome Letter/Onboarding started?	
Notes:		

HCA Health Care	Avg. 30k-$80k	https://careers.hcahealthcare.com/
Yes/No	Job offered in your state and hiring?	
	What salary amount is offered?	
Yes/No	Do you like the opportunity, rate 1-5	
Yes/No	Resume/Cover letter sent/date	
Yes/No	Was the interview/Assessment Completed?	
Yes/No	Welcome Letter/Onboarding started?	
Notes:		

Head Space	Avg. 40k-$60k	https://www.headspace.com/join-us
Yes/No	Job offered in your state and hiring?	
	What salary amount is offered?	
Yes/No	Do you like the opportunity, rate 1-5	
Yes/No	Resume/Cover letter sent/date	
Yes/No	Was the interview/Assessment Completed?	
Yes/No	Welcome Letter/Onboarding started?	
Notes:		

Health Advocate	Avg. 40k-$60k	https://www.healthadvocate.com/site/careers
Yes/No	Job offered in your state and hiring?	
	What salary amount is offered?	
Yes/No	Do you like the opportunity, rate 1-5	
Yes/No	Resume/Cover letter sent/date	
Yes/No	Was the interview/Assessment Completed?	
Yes/No	Welcome Letter/Onboarding started?	
Notes:		

Highmark Health	Avg. 30k-$70k	https://careers.highmarkhealth.org/
Yes/No	Job offered in your state and hiring?	
	What salary amount is offered?	
Yes/No	Do you like the opportunity, rate 1-5	
Yes/No	Resume/Cover letter sent/date	
Yes/No	Was the interview/Assessment Completed?	
Yes/No	Welcome Letter/Onboarding started?	
Notes:		

Home Chef	Avg. 30k-$40k	https://www.homechef.com/careers
Yes/No	Job offered in your state and hiring?	
	What salary amount is offered?	
Yes/No	Do you like the opportunity, rate 1-5	
Yes/No	Resume/Cover letter sent/date	
Yes/No	Was the interview/Assessment Completed?	
Yes/No	Welcome Letter/Onboarding started?	
Notes:		

Home Site	Avg. 40k-$50k	https://go.homesite.com/career
Yes/No	Job offered in your state and hiring?	
	What salary amount is offered?	
Yes/No	Do you like the opportunity, rate 1-5	
Yes/No	Resume/Cover letter sent/date	
Yes/No	Was the interview/Assessment Completed?	
Yes/No	Welcome Letter/Onboarding started?	
Notes:		

Honor Health	Avg. 30k-$100k	https://jobs.honorhealth.com/
Yes/No	Job offered in your state and hiring?	
	What salary amount is offered?	
Yes/No	Do you like the opportunity, rate 1-5	
Yes/No	Resume/Cover letter sent/date	
Yes/No	Was the interview/Assessment Completed?	
Yes/No	Welcome Letter/Onboarding started?	
Notes:		

Housecall Pro	Avg. 40k-$60k	https://www.housecallpro.com/careers/
Yes/No	Job offered in your state and hiring?	
	What salary amount is offered?	
Yes/No	Do you like the opportunity, rate 1-5	
Yes/No	Resume/Cover letter sent/date	
Yes/No	Was the interview/Assessment Completed?	
Yes/No	Welcome Letter/Onboarding started?	
Notes:		

Humana	Avg. 40k-$60k	https://careers.humana.com/
Yes/No	Job offered in your state and hiring?	
	What salary amount is offered?	
Yes/No	Do you like the opportunity, rate 1-5	
Yes/No	Resume/Cover letter sent/date	
Yes/No	Was the interview/Assessment Completed?	
Yes/No	Welcome Letter/Onboarding started?	
Notes:		

Hyatt Hotel	Avg. 30k-$40k	https://careers.hyatt.com/en-US/careers/
Yes/No	Job offered in your state and hiring?	
	What salary amount is offered?	
Yes/No	Do you like the opportunity, rate 1-5	
Yes/No	Resume/Cover letter sent/date	
Yes/No	Was the interview/Assessment Completed?	
Yes/No	Welcome Letter/Onboarding started?	
Notes:		

Iherb	Avg. 40k-$60k	https://careers.iherb.com/global/en/
Yes/No	Job offered in your state and hiring?	
	What salary amount is offered?	
Yes/No	Do you like the opportunity, rate 1-5	
Yes/No	Resume/Cover letter sent/date	
Yes/No	Was the interview/Assessment Completed?	
Yes/No	Welcome Letter/Onboarding started?	
Notes:		

Imagen	Avg. 40k-$60k	https://imagen.ai/careers/
Yes/No	Job offered in your state and hiring?	
	What salary amount is offered?	
Yes/No	Do you like the opportunity, rate 1-5	
Yes/No	Resume/Cover letter sent/date	
Yes/No	Was the interview/Assessment Completed?	
Yes/No	Welcome Letter/Onboarding started?	
Notes:		

Imiweb.com	Avg. 48k-$80k	https://imiweb.com/careers/
Yes/No	Job offered in your state and hiring?	
	What salary amount is offered?	
Yes/No	Do you like the opportunity, rate 1-5	
Yes/No	Resume/Cover letter sent/date	
Yes/No	Was the interview/Assessment Completed?	
Yes/No	Welcome Letter/Onboarding started?	
Notes:		

Indiana Farmers Ins.	Avg. 40k-$60k	https://www.indianafarmers.com/about-us/careers
Yes/No	Job offered in your state and hiring?	
	What salary amount is offered?	
Yes/No	Do you like the opportunity, rate 1-5	
Yes/No	Resume/Cover letter sent/date	
Yes/No	Was the interview/Assessment Completed?	
Yes/No	Welcome Letter/Onboarding started?	
Notes:		

Infocision	Avg. 30k-$60k	https://www.infocision.com/wah/
Yes/No	Job offered in your state and hiring?	
	What salary amount is offered?	
Yes/No	Do you like the opportunity, rate 1-5	
Yes/No	Resume/Cover letter sent/date	
Yes/No	Was the interview/Assessment Completed?	
Yes/No	Welcome Letter/Onboarding started?	
Notes:		

Innosource	Avg. 40k-$60k	https://innosource.jobs.net/
Yes/No	Job offered in your state and hiring?	
	What salary amount is offered?	
Yes/No	Do you like the opportunity, rate 1-5	
Yes/No	Resume/Cover letter sent/date	
Yes/No	Was the interview/Assessment Completed?	
Yes/No	Welcome Letter/Onboarding started?	
Notes:		

Insurity	Avg. 30k-$60k	https://jobs.jobvite.com/insurity/
Yes/No	Job offered in your state and hiring?	
	What salary amount is offered?	
Yes/No	Do you like the opportunity, rate 1-5	
Yes/No	Resume/Cover letter sent/date	
Yes/No	Was the interview/Assessment Completed?	
Yes/No	Welcome Letter/Onboarding started?	
Notes:		

Intel Corporations	Avg. 38k-$60k	https://jobs.intel.com/en
Yes/No	Job offered in your state and hiring?	
	What salary amount is offered?	
Yes/No	Do you like the opportunity, rate 1-5	
Yes/No	Resume/Cover letter sent/date	
Yes/No	Was the interview/Assessment Completed?	
Yes/No	Welcome Letter/Onboarding started?	
Notes:		

Intouch CX	Avg. 30k-$50k	https://www.intouchcx.com/careers/
Yes/No	Job offered in your state and hiring?	
	What salary amount is offered?	
Yes/No	Do you like the opportunity, rate 1-5	
Yes/No	Resume/Cover letter sent/date	
Yes/No	Was the interview/Assessment Completed?	
Yes/No	Welcome Letter/Onboarding started?	
Notes:		

Intoxalock	Avg. 50k-$60k	https://www.intoxalock.com/about/careers/
Yes/No	Job offered in your state and hiring?	
	What salary amount is offered?	
Yes/No	Do you like the opportunity, rate 1-5	
Yes/No	Resume/Cover letter sent/date	
Yes/No	Was the interview/Assessment Completed?	
Yes/No	Welcome Letter/Onboarding started?	
Notes:		

IQOR	Avg. 30k-$40k	https://jobs.iqor.com/	
Yes/No	Job offered in your state and hiring?		
	What salary amount is offered?		
Yes/No	Do you like the opportunity, rate 1-5		
Yes/No	Resume/Cover letter sent/date		
Yes/No	Was the interview/Assessment Completed?		
Yes/No	Welcome Letter/Onboarding started?		
Notes:			

IQVIA	Avg. 30k-$60k	https://jobs.iqvia.com/	
Yes/No	Job offered in your state and hiring?		
	What salary amount is offered?		
Yes/No	Do you like the opportunity, rate 1-5		
Yes/No	Resume/Cover letter sent/date		
Yes/No	Was the interview/Assessment Completed?		
Yes/No	Welcome Letter/Onboarding started?		
Notes:			

IRS	Avg. 50k-$60k	https://www.jobs.irs.gov/	
Yes/No	Job offered in your state and hiring?		
	What salary amount is offered?		
Yes/No	Do you like the opportunity, rate 1-5		
Yes/No	Resume/Cover letter sent/date		
Yes/No	Was the interview/Assessment Completed?		
Yes/No	Welcome Letter/Onboarding started?		
Notes:			

Jabra GN	Avg. 40k-$60k	jabra.com/about/careers
Yes/No	Job offered in your state and hiring?	
	What salary amount is offered?	
Yes/No	Do you like the opportunity, rate 1-5	
Yes/No	Resume/Cover letter sent/date	
Yes/No	Was the interview/Assessment Completed?	
Yes/No	Welcome Letter/Onboarding started?	
Notes:		

8 COMPANIES K-M

Kaiser Permanente	Avg. 30k-$60k	https://www.kaiserpermanentejobs.org/
Yes/No	Job offered in your state and hiring?	
	What salary amount is offered?	
Yes/No	Do you like the opportunity, rate 1-5	
Yes/No	Resume/Cover letter sent/date	
Yes/No	Was the interview/Assessment Completed?	
Yes/No	Welcome Letter/Onboarding started?	
Notes:		

Kindbody Medical Biller	Avg. 30k-$60k	https://kindbody.com/careers/
Yes/No	Job offered in your state and hiring?	
	What salary amount is offered?	
Yes/No	Do you like the opportunity, rate 1-5	
Yes/No	Resume/Cover letter sent/date	
Yes/No	Was the interview/Assessment Completed?	
Yes/No	Welcome Letter/Onboarding started?	
Notes:		

Lap of Love	Avg. 30k-$70k	https://info.lapoflove.com/jobs
Yes/No	Job offered in your state and hiring?	
	What salary amount is offered?	
Yes/No	Do you like the opportunity, rate 1-5	
Yes/No	Resume/Cover letter sent/date	
Yes/No	Was the interview/Assessment Completed?	
Yes/No	Welcome Letter/Onboarding started?	
Notes:		

Liberty Mutual	Avg. 30k-$60k	https://www.libertymutualgroup.com/about-lm/careers/overview
Yes/No	Job offered in your state and hiring?	
	What salary amount is offered?	
Yes/No	Do you like the opportunity, rate 1-5	
Yes/No	Resume/Cover letter sent/date	
Yes/No	Was the interview/Assessment Completed?	
Yes/No	Welcome Letter/Onboarding started?	
Notes:		

Lincoln Financial	Avg. 40k-$100k	https://jobs.lincolnfinancial.com/
Yes/No	Job offered in your state and hiring?	
	What salary amount is offered?	
Yes/No	Do you like the opportunity, rate 1-5	
Yes/No	Resume/Cover letter sent/date	
Yes/No	Was the interview/Assessment Completed?	
Yes/No	Welcome Letter/Onboarding started?	
Notes:		

Live Nation Ent.	Avg. 30k-$60k	https://www.livenationentertainment.com/careers/
Yes/No	Job offered in your state and hiring?	
	What salary amount is offered?	
Yes/No	Do you like the opportunity, rate 1-5	
Yes/No	Resume/Cover letter sent/date	
Yes/No	Was the interview/Assessment Completed?	
Yes/No	Welcome Letter/Onboarding started?	
Notes:		

Live Ops	Avg. 30k-$60k	https://join.liveops.com/
Yes/No	Job offered in your state and hiring?	
	What salary amount is offered?	
Yes/No	Do you like the opportunity, rate 1-5	
Yes/No	Resume/Cover letter sent/date	
Yes/No	Was the interview/Assessment Completed?	
Yes/No	Welcome Letter/Onboarding started?	
Notes:		

Loan Care	Avg. 30k-$60k	https://www.loancareservicing.com/about-us/careers/
Yes/No	Job offered in your state and hiring?	
	What salary amount is offered?	
Yes/No	Do you like the opportunity, rate 1-5	
Yes/No	Resume/Cover letter sent/date	
Yes/No	Was the interview/Assessment Completed?	
Yes/No	Welcome Letter/Onboarding started?	
Notes:		

Loan Depot	Avg. 30k-$160k	https://jobs.jobvite.com/loandepot/
Yes/No	Job offered in your state and hiring?	
	What salary amount is offered?	
Yes/No	Do you like the opportunity, rate 1-5	
Yes/No	Resume/Cover letter sent/date	
Yes/No	Was the interview/Assessment Completed?	
Yes/No	Welcome Letter/Onboarding started?	
Notes:		

Loom	Avg. 30k-$60k	https://www.loom.com/careers
Yes/No	Job offered in your state and hiring?	
	What salary amount is offered?	
Yes/No	Do you like the opportunity, rate 1-5	
Yes/No	Resume/Cover letter sent/date	
Yes/No	Was the interview/Assessment Completed?	
Yes/No	Welcome Letter/Onboarding started?	
Notes:		

Lumen	Avg. 30k-$60k	https://jobs.lumen.com/global/en
Yes/No	Job offered in your state and hiring?	
	What salary amount is offered?	
Yes/No	Do you like the opportunity, rate 1-5	
Yes/No	Resume/Cover letter sent/date	
Yes/No	Was the interview/Assessment Completed?	
Yes/No	Welcome Letter/Onboarding started?	
Notes:		

Marriott	Avg. 30k-$60k	https://careers.marriott.com/
Yes/No	Job offered in your state and hiring?	
	What salary amount is offered?	
Yes/No	Do you like the opportunity, rate 1-5	
Yes/No	Resume/Cover letter sent/date	
Yes/No	Was the interview/Assessment Completed?	
Yes/No	Welcome Letter/Onboarding started?	
Notes:		

Master Lock	Avg. 30k-$60k	https://careers.smartrecruiters.com/FortuneBrands/master-lock
Yes/No	Job offered in your state and hiring?	
	What salary amount is offered?	
Yes/No	Do you like the opportunity, rate 1-5	
Yes/No	Resume/Cover letter sent/date	
Yes/No	Was the interview/Assessment Completed?	
Yes/No	Welcome Letter/Onboarding started?	
Notes:		

Mattress Firm	Avg. 30k-$60k	https://www.mattressfirm.com/mattress-firm-careers
Yes/No	Job offered in your state and hiring?	
	What salary amount is offered?	
Yes/No	Do you like the opportunity, rate 1-5	
Yes/No	Resume/Cover letter sent/date	
Yes/No	Was the interview/Assessment Completed?	
Yes/No	Welcome Letter/Onboarding started?	
Notes:		

Maximus	Avg. 30k-$60k	https://maximus.com/careers
Yes/No	Job offered in your state and hiring?	
	What salary amount is offered?	
Yes/No	Do you like the opportunity, rate 1-5	
Yes/No	Resume/Cover letter sent/date	
Yes/No	Was the interview/Assessment Completed?	
Yes/No	Welcome Letter/Onboarding started?	
Notes:		

Mayo Clinic	Avg. 40k-$60k	https://jobs.mayoclinic.org/remote
Yes/No	Job offered in your state and hiring?	
	What salary amount is offered?	
Yes/No	Do you like the opportunity, rate 1-5	
Yes/No	Resume/Cover letter sent/date	
Yes/No	Was the interview/Assessment Completed?	
Yes/No	Welcome Letter/Onboarding started?	
Notes:		

McKesson Corp.	Avg. 35k-$60k	https://careers.mckesson.com/en
Yes/No	Job offered in your state and hiring?	
	What salary amount is offered?	
Yes/No	Do you like the opportunity, rate 1-5	
Yes/No	Resume/Cover letter sent/date	
Yes/No	Was the interview/Assessment Completed?	
Yes/No	Welcome Letter/Onboarding started?	
Notes:		

MCRA	Avg. 30k-$60k	https://www.mcra.com/about-us/our-team/careers
Yes/No	Job offered in your state and hiring?	
	What salary amount is offered?	
Yes/No	Do you like the opportunity, rate 1-5	
Yes/No	Resume/Cover letter sent/date	
Yes/No	Was the interview/Assessment Completed?	
Yes/No	Welcome Letter/Onboarding started?	
Notes:		

MDS Comm.	Avg. 30k-$50k	https://www.mdscom.com/careers
Yes/No	Job offered in your state and hiring?	
	What salary amount is offered?	
Yes/No	Do you like the opportunity, rate 1-5	
Yes/No	Resume/Cover letter sent/date	
Yes/No	Was the interview/Assessment Completed?	
Yes/No	Welcome Letter/Onboarding started?	
Notes:		

Mercy Health	Avg. 30k-$60k	https://www.mercy.com/about-us/careers
Yes/No	Job offered in your state and hiring?	
	What salary amount is offered?	
Yes/No	Do you like the opportunity, rate 1-5	
Yes/No	Resume/Cover letter sent/date	
Yes/No	Was the interview/Assessment Completed?	
Yes/No	Welcome Letter/Onboarding started?	
Notes:		

Metlife	Avg. 40k-$60k	https://jobs.metlife.com/
Yes/No	Job offered in your state and hiring?	
	What salary amount is offered?	
Yes/No	Do you like the opportunity, rate 1-5	
Yes/No	Resume/Cover letter sent/date	
Yes/No	Was the interview/Assessment Completed?	
Yes/No	Welcome Letter/Onboarding started?	
Notes:		

Metrix Learning	Avg. 50k-$80k	https://metrixlearning.com/workforce/
Yes/No	Job offered in your state and hiring?	
	What salary amount is offered?	
Yes/No	Do you like the opportunity, rate 1-5	
Yes/No	Resume/Cover letter sent/date	
Yes/No	Was the interview/Assessment Completed?	
Yes/No	Welcome Letter/Onboarding started?	
Notes:		

Mobile at Snap	Avg. 40k-$60k	https://www.snapraise.com/careers/
Yes/No	Job offered in your state and hiring?	
	What salary amount is offered?	
Yes/No	Do you like the opportunity, rate 1-5	
Yes/No	Resume/Cover letter sent/date	
Yes/No	Was the interview/Assessment Completed?	
Yes/No	Welcome Letter/Onboarding started?	
Notes:		

Molina	Avg. 30k-$60k	https://careers.molinahealthcare.com/
Yes/No	Job offered in your state and hiring?	
	What salary amount is offered?	
Yes/No	Do you like the opportunity, rate 1-5	
Yes/No	Resume/Cover letter sent/date	
Yes/No	Was the interview/Assessment Completed?	
Yes/No	Welcome Letter/Onboarding started?	
Notes:		

Motion Global	Avg. 30k-$60k	jobs.motionglobal.com/
Yes/No	Job offered in your state and hiring?	
	What salary amount is offered?	
Yes/No	Do you like the opportunity, rate 1-5	
Yes/No	Resume/Cover letter sent/date	
Yes/No	Was the interview/Assessment Completed?	
Yes/No	Welcome Letter/Onboarding started?	
Notes:		

Mudflap	Avg. 38k-$60k	https://www.mudflapinc.com/careers
Yes/No	Job offered in your state and hiring?	
	What salary amount is offered?	
Yes/No	Do you like the opportunity, rate 1-5	
Yes/No	Resume/Cover letter sent/date	
Yes/No	Was the interview/Assessment Completed?	
Yes/No	Welcome Letter/Onboarding started?	
Notes:		

Mutual of Omaha	Avg. 38k-$60k	https://www.mutualofomaha.com/careers/
Yes/No	Job offered in your state and hiring?	
	What salary amount is offered?	
Yes/No	Do you like the opportunity, rate 1-5	
Yes/No	Resume/Cover letter sent/date	
Yes/No	Was the interview/Assessment Completed?	
Yes/No	Welcome Letter/Onboarding started?	
Notes:		

My Kelly	Avg. 38k-$60k	https://www.mykelly.com/
Yes/No	Job offered in your state and hiring?	
	What salary amount is offered?	
Yes/No	Do you like the opportunity, rate 1-5	
Yes/No	Resume/Cover letter sent/date	
Yes/No	Was the interview/Assessment Completed?	
Yes/No	Welcome Letter/Onboarding started?	
Notes:		

9 COMPANIES N-P

Natera	Avg. 33k-$40k	https://www.natera.com/company/careers/
Yes/No	Job offered in your state and hiring?	
	What salary amount is offered?	
Yes/No	Do you like the opportunity, rate 1-5	
Yes/No	Resume/Cover letter sent/date	
Yes/No	Was the interview/Assessment Completed?	
Yes/No	Welcome Letter/Onboarding started?	
Notes:		

National General Ins.	Avg. 38k-$50k	https://careers.nationalgeneral.com/
Yes/No	Job offered in your state and hiring?	
	What salary amount is offered?	
Yes/No	Do you like the opportunity, rate 1-5	
Yes/No	Resume/Cover letter sent/date	
Yes/No	Was the interview/Assessment Completed?	
Yes/No	Welcome Letter/Onboarding started?	
Notes:		

National Guardian Life	Avg. 40k-$120k	https://www.nglic.com/Careers
Yes/No	Job offered in your state and hiring?	
	What salary amount is offered?	
Yes/No	Do you like the opportunity, rate 1-5	
Yes/No	Resume/Cover letter sent/date	
Yes/No	Was the interview/Assessment Completed?	
Yes/No	Welcome Letter/Onboarding started?	
Notes:		

Nationwide	Avg. 30k-$50k	https://www.nationwide.com/personal/about-us/careers/
Yes/No	Job offered in your state and hiring?	
	What salary amount is offered?	
Yes/No	Do you like the opportunity, rate 1-5	
Yes/No	Resume/Cover letter sent/date	
Yes/No	Was the interview/Assessment Completed?	
Yes/No	Welcome Letter/Onboarding started?	
Notes:		

Navienet	Avg. 30k-$60k	https://jobs.navient.com/
Yes/No	Job offered in your state and hiring?	
	What salary amount is offered?	
Yes/No	Do you like the opportunity, rate 1-5	
Yes/No	Resume/Cover letter sent/date	
Yes/No	Was the interview/Assessment Completed?	
Yes/No	Welcome Letter/Onboarding started?	
Notes:		

Neighbors Bank	Avg. 48k-$60k	https://www.neighborsbank.com/careers/
Yes/No	Job offered in your state and hiring?	
	What salary amount is offered?	
Yes/No	Do you like the opportunity, rate 1-5	
Yes/No	Resume/Cover letter sent/date	
Yes/No	Was the interview/Assessment Completed?	
Yes/No	Welcome Letter/Onboarding started?	
Notes:		

Nerd Wallet	Avg. 38k-$60k	https://www.nerdwallet.com/careers
Yes/No	Job offered in your state and hiring?	
	What salary amount is offered?	
Yes/No	Do you like the opportunity, rate 1-5	
Yes/No	Resume/Cover letter sent/date	
Yes/No	Was the interview/Assessment Completed?	
Yes/No	Welcome Letter/Onboarding started?	
Notes:		

NexRep	Avg. 30k-$50k	https://nexrep.com/agents
Yes/No	Job offered in your state and hiring?	
	What salary amount is offered?	
Yes/No	Do you like the opportunity, rate 1-5	
Yes/No	Resume/Cover letter sent/date	
Yes/No	Was the interview/Assessment Completed?	
Yes/No	Welcome Letter/Onboarding started?	
Notes:		

Nordstrom	Avg. 44k-$60k	https://careers.nordstrom.com/
Yes/No	Job offered in your state and hiring?	
	What salary amount is offered?	
Yes/No	Do you like the opportunity, rate 1-5	
Yes/No	Resume/Cover letter sent/date	
Yes/No	Was the interview/Assessment Completed?	
Yes/No	Welcome Letter/Onboarding started?	
Notes:		

Oak St. Health	Avg. 38k-$60k	https://www.oakstreethealth.com/careers
Yes/No	Job offered in your state and hiring?	
	What salary amount is offered?	
Yes/No	Do you like the opportunity, rate 1-5	
Yes/No	Resume/Cover letter sent/date	
Yes/No	Was the interview/Assessment Completed?	
Yes/No	Welcome Letter/Onboarding started?	
Notes:		

Ollie Pets	Avg. 30k-$60k	https://jobs.lever.co/myollie
Yes/No	Job offered in your state and hiring?	
	What salary amount is offered?	
Yes/No	Do you like the opportunity, rate 1-5	
Yes/No	Resume/Cover letter sent/date	
Yes/No	Was the interview/Assessment Completed?	
Yes/No	Welcome Letter/Onboarding started?	
Notes:		

Omada Health	Avg. 30k-$60k	https://www.omadahealth.com/about-us/careers
Yes/No	Job offered in your state and hiring?	
	What salary amount is offered?	
Yes/No	Do you like the opportunity, rate 1-5	
Yes/No	Resume/Cover letter sent/date	
Yes/No	Was the interview/Assessment Completed?	
Yes/No	Welcome Letter/Onboarding started?	
Notes:		

Omni Interactions	Avg. 38k-$60k	https://omniinteractions.com/
Yes/No	Job offered in your state and hiring?	
	What salary amount is offered?	
Yes/No	Do you like the opportunity, rate 1-5	
Yes/No	Resume/Cover letter sent/date	
Yes/No	Was the interview/Assessment Completed?	
Yes/No	Welcome Letter/Onboarding started?	
Notes:		

One Call Navigator	Avg. 38k-$60k	https://onecallcm.com/about/careers/
Yes/No	Job offered in your state and hiring?	
	What salary amount is offered?	
Yes/No	Do you like the opportunity, rate 1-5	
Yes/No	Resume/Cover letter sent/date	
Yes/No	Was the interview/Assessment Completed?	
Yes/No	Welcome Letter/Onboarding started?	
Notes:		

Ontra	Avg. 80k-$160k	https://www.ontra.ai/careers/
Yes/No	Job offered in your state and hiring?	
	What salary amount is offered?	
Yes/No	Do you like the opportunity, rate 1-5	
Yes/No	Resume/Cover letter sent/date	
Yes/No	Was the interview/Assessment Completed?	
Yes/No	Welcome Letter/Onboarding started?	
Notes:		

OppFI	Avg. 38k-$60k	https://www.oppfi.com/careers/
Yes/No	Job offered in your state and hiring?	
	What salary amount is offered?	
Yes/No	Do you like the opportunity, rate 1-5	
Yes/No	Resume/Cover letter sent/date	
Yes/No	Was the interview/Assessment Completed?	
Yes/No	Welcome Letter/Onboarding started?	
Notes:		

Optum Pharmacy	Avg. 38k-$60k	https://www.optum.com/careers.html
Yes/No	Job offered in your state and hiring?	
	What salary amount is offered?	
Yes/No	Do you like the opportunity, rate 1-5	
Yes/No	Resume/Cover letter sent/date	
Yes/No	Was the interview/Assessment Completed?	
Yes/No	Welcome Letter/Onboarding started?	
Notes:		

Overstock	Avg. 38k-$60k	https://www.indeed.com/overstock
Yes/No	Job offered in your state and hiring?	
	What salary amount is offered?	
Yes/No	Do you like the opportunity, rate 1-5	
Yes/No	Resume/Cover letter sent/date	
Yes/No	Was the interview/Assessment Completed?	
Yes/No	Welcome Letter/Onboarding started?	
Notes:		

Oz Net	Avg. 38k-$60k	https://www.indeed.com/cmp/Oz-Net
Yes/No	Job offered in your state and hiring?	
	What salary amount is offered?	
Yes/No	Do you like the opportunity, rate 1-5	
Yes/No	Resume/Cover letter sent/date	
Yes/No	Was the interview/Assessment Completed?	
Yes/No	Welcome Letter/Onboarding started?	
Notes:		

Pacific Life	Avg. 48k-$60k	https://www.pacificlife.com/home/Careers.html
Yes/No	Job offered in your state and hiring?	
	What salary amount is offered?	
Yes/No	Do you like the opportunity, rate 1-5	
Yes/No	Resume/Cover letter sent/date	
Yes/No	Was the interview/Assessment Completed?	
Yes/No	Welcome Letter/Onboarding started?	
Notes:		

Paramount Staffing	Avg. 38k-$60k	https://www.hireparamount.com/
Yes/No	Job offered in your state and hiring?	
	What salary amount is offered?	
Yes/No	Do you like the opportunity, rate 1-5	
Yes/No	Resume/Cover letter sent/date	
Yes/No	Was the interview/Assessment Completed?	
Yes/No	Welcome Letter/Onboarding started?	
Notes:		

Parchment	Avg. 34k-$60k	https://www.parchment.com/company/careers/
Yes/No	Job offered in your state and hiring?	
	What salary amount is offered?	
Yes/No	Do you like the opportunity, rate 1-5	
Yes/No	Resume/Cover letter sent/date	
Yes/No	Was the interview/Assessment Completed?	
Yes/No	Welcome Letter/Onboarding started?	
Notes:		

Pay Common Line	Avg. 30k-$60k	https://www.paycom.com/careers/
Yes/No	Job offered in your state and hiring?	
	What salary amount is offered?	
Yes/No	Do you like the opportunity, rate 1-5	
Yes/No	Resume/Cover letter sent/date	
Yes/No	Was the interview/Assessment Completed?	
Yes/No	Welcome Letter/Onboarding started?	
Notes:		

Paylocity	Avg. 30k-$48k	ttps://www.paylocity.com/careers/
Yes/No	Job offered in your state and hiring?	
	What salary amount is offered?	
Yes/No	Do you like the opportunity, rate 1-5	
Yes/No	Resume/Cover letter sent/date	
Yes/No	Was the interview/Assessment Completed?	
Yes/No	Welcome Letter/Onboarding started?	
Notes:		

People Share	Avg. 38k-$60k	https://www.peopleshareworks.com/careers-at-peopleshare/
Yes/No	Job offered in your state and hiring?	
	What salary amount is offered?	
Yes/No	Do you like the opportunity, rate 1-5	
Yes/No	Resume/Cover letter sent/date	
Yes/No	Was the interview/Assessment Completed?	
Yes/No	Welcome Letter/Onboarding started?	
Notes:		

PetSmart	Avg. 30k-$60k	https://careers.petsmart.com/
Yes/No	Job offered in your state and hiring?	
	What salary amount is offered?	
Yes/No	Do you like the opportunity, rate 1-5	
Yes/No	Resume/Cover letter sent/date	
Yes/No	Was the interview/Assessment Completed?	
Yes/No	Welcome Letter/Onboarding started?	
Notes:		

Pharmacy Tech	Avg. 38k-$60k	https://www.indeed.com/pharmacytech Need a Certificate
Yes/No	Job offered in your state and hiring?	
	What salary amount is offered?	
Yes/No	Do you like the opportunity, rate 1-5	
Yes/No	Resume/Cover letter sent/date	
Yes/No	Was the interview/Assessment Completed?	
Yes/No	Welcome Letter/Onboarding started?	
Notes:		

Phillips Health Care	Avg. 38k-$60k	https://www.careers.philips.com/na/en
Yes/No	Job offered in your state and hiring?	
	What salary amount is offered?	
Yes/No	Do you like the opportunity, rate 1-5	
Yes/No	Resume/Cover letter sent/date	
Yes/No	Was the interview/Assessment Completed?	
Yes/No	Welcome Letter/Onboarding started?	
Notes:		

Piedomont Health Care	Avg. 30k-$60k	https://piedmontcareers.org/
Yes/No	Job offered in your state and hiring?	
	What salary amount is offered?	
Yes/No	Do you like the opportunity, rate 1-5	
Yes/No	Resume/Cover letter sent/date	
Yes/No	Was the interview/Assessment Completed?	
Yes/No	Welcome Letter/Onboarding started?	
Notes:		

PNC	Avg. 34k-$60k	https://careers.pnc.com/global/en
Yes/No	Job offered in your state and hiring?	
	What salary amount is offered?	
Yes/No	Do you like the opportunity, rate 1-5	
Yes/No	Resume/Cover letter sent/date	
Yes/No	Was the interview/Assessment Completed?	
Yes/No	Welcome Letter/Onboarding started?	
Notes:		

Pop Health Care	Avg. 34k-$60k	https://www.indeed.com/cmp/Pophealth care-LLC/topics/work-from-home
Yes/No	Job offered in your state and hiring?	
	What salary amount is offered?	
Yes/No	Do you like the opportunity, rate 1-5	
Yes/No	Resume/Cover letter sent/date	
Yes/No	Was the interview/Assessment Completed?	
Yes/No	Welcome Letter/Onboarding started?	
Notes:		

Progressive	Avg. 34k-$60k	https://www.progressive.com/careers/differ ence/work-from-home/
Yes/No	Job offered in your state and hiring?	
	What salary amount is offered?	
Yes/No	Do you like the opportunity, rate 1-5	
Yes/No	Resume/Cover letter sent/date	
Yes/No	Was the interview/Assessment Completed?	
Yes/No	Welcome Letter/Onboarding started?	
Notes:		

Prudential	Avg. 44k-$160k	https://jobs.prudential.com/
Yes/No	Job offered in your state and hiring?	
	What salary amount is offered?	
Yes/No	Do you like the opportunity, rate 1-5	
Yes/No	Resume/Cover letter sent/date	
Yes/No	Was the interview/Assessment Completed?	
Yes/No	Welcome Letter/Onboarding started?	
Notes:		

PSCU	Avg. 32k-$160k	https://www.pscu.com/careers
Yes/No	Job offered in your state and hiring?	
	What salary amount is offered?	
Yes/No	Do you like the opportunity, rate 1-5	
Yes/No	Resume/Cover letter sent/date	
Yes/No	Was the interview/Assessment Completed?	
Yes/No	Welcome Letter/Onboarding started?	
Notes:		

Public Storage	Avg. 30k-$160k	https://www.publicstoragejobs.com/
Yes/No	Job offered in your state and hiring?	
	What salary amount is offered?	
Yes/No	Do you like the opportunity, rate 1-5	
Yes/No	Resume/Cover letter sent/date	
Yes/No	Was the interview/Assessment Completed?	
Yes/No	Welcome Letter/Onboarding started?	
Notes:		

Publishing.com	Avg. 44k-$60k	https://www.publishing.com/careers
Yes/No	Job offered in your state and hiring?	
	What salary amount is offered?	
Yes/No	Do you like the opportunity, rate 1-5	
Yes/No	Resume/Cover letter sent/date	
Yes/No	Was the interview/Assessment Completed?	
Yes/No	Welcome Letter/Onboarding started?	
Notes:		

10 COMPANIES Q-S

Qualfon	Avg. 30k-$60k	https://careers.qualfon.com/
Yes/No	Job offered in your state and hiring?	
	What salary amount is offered?	
Yes/No	Do you like the opportunity, rate 1-5	
Yes/No	Resume/Cover letter sent/date	
Yes/No	Was the interview/Assessment Completed?	
Yes/No	Welcome Letter/Onboarding started?	
Notes:		

Quick Med Claims	Avg. 33k-$60k	https://www.quickmedclaims.com/careers/
Yes/No	Job offered in your state and hiring?	
	What salary amount is offered?	
Yes/No	Do you like the opportunity, rate 1-5	
Yes/No	Resume/Cover letter sent/date	
Yes/No	Was the interview/Assessment Completed?	
Yes/No	Welcome Letter/Onboarding started?	
Notes:		

Qulfon	Avg. 30k-$60k	https://careers.qualfon.com/go/Work-at-Home-Representative-Jobs/
Yes/No	Job offered in your state and hiring?	
	What salary amount is offered?	
Yes/No	Do you like the opportunity, rate 1-5	
Yes/No	Resume/Cover letter sent/date	
Yes/No	Was the interview/Assessment Completed?	
Yes/No	Welcome Letter/Onboarding started?	
Notes:		

Qurate Retail Group	Avg. 30k-$60k	https://careers.qurateretailgroup.com/
Yes/No	Job offered in your state and hiring?	
	What salary amount is offered?	
Yes/No	Do you like the opportunity, rate 1-5	
Yes/No	Resume/Cover letter sent/date	
Yes/No	Was the interview/Assessment Completed?	
Yes/No	Welcome Letter/Onboarding started?	
Notes:		

QVC	Avg. 30k-$60k	https://careers.qurateretailgroup.com/qvc-us/
Yes/No	Job offered in your state and hiring?	
	What salary amount is offered?	
Yes/No	Do you like the opportunity, rate 1-5	
Yes/No	Resume/Cover letter sent/date	
Yes/No	Was the interview/Assessment Completed?	
Yes/No	Welcome Letter/Onboarding started?	
Notes:		

Ramsay Health Care	Avg. 64k-$80k	https://www.ramsayhealth.com/en/people-and-careers/job-search/
Yes/No	Job offered in your state and hiring?	
	What salary amount is offered?	
Yes/No	Do you like the opportunity, rate 1-5	
Yes/No	Resume/Cover letter sent/date	
Yes/No	Was the interview/Assessment Completed?	
Yes/No	Welcome Letter/Onboarding started?	
Notes:		

Ranstad	Avg. 34k-$60k	https://www.randstadusa.com/careers-at-randstad/
Yes/No	Job offered in your state and hiring?	
	What salary amount is offered?	
Yes/No	Do you like the opportunity, rate 1-5	
Yes/No	Resume/Cover letter sent/date	
Yes/No	Was the interview/Assessment Completed?	
Yes/No	Welcome Letter/Onboarding started?	
Notes:		

Refer CX Results	Avg. 30k-$60k	https://careers.resultscx.com/
Yes/No	Job offered in your state and hiring?	
	What salary amount is offered?	
Yes/No	Do you like the opportunity, rate 1-5	
Yes/No	Resume/Cover letter sent/date	
Yes/No	Was the interview/Assessment Completed?	
Yes/No	Welcome Letter/Onboarding started?	
Notes:		

Rent a Center	Avg. 30k-$60k	https://raccareers.com/
Yes/No	Job offered in your state and hiring?	
	What salary amount is offered?	
Yes/No	Do you like the opportunity, rate 1-5	
Yes/No	Resume/Cover letter sent/date	
Yes/No	Was the interview/Assessment Completed?	
Yes/No	Welcome Letter/Onboarding started?	
Notes:		

Roadie	Avg. 38k-$60k	https://www.roadie.com/careers-culture
Yes/No	Job offered in your state and hiring?	
	What salary amount is offered?	
Yes/No	Do you like the opportunity, rate 1-5	
Yes/No	Resume/Cover letter sent/date	
Yes/No	Was the interview/Assessment Completed?	
Yes/No	Welcome Letter/Onboarding started?	
Notes:		

Rothman Orthopaedics	Avg. 36k-$60k	https://rothmanortho.com/about-us/careers/
Yes/No	Job offered in your state and hiring?	
	What salary amount is offered?	
Yes/No	Do you like the opportunity, rate 1-5	
Yes/No	Resume/Cover letter sent/date	
Yes/No	Was the interview/Assessment Completed?	
Yes/No	Welcome Letter/Onboarding started?	
Notes:		

SafeLite Auto Glass	Avg. 30k-$60k	https://www.safelite.com/careers
Yes/No	Job offered in your state and hiring?	
	What salary amount is offered?	
Yes/No	Do you like the opportunity, rate 1-5	
Yes/No	Resume/Cover letter sent/date	
Yes/No	Was the interview/Assessment Completed?	
Yes/No	Welcome Letter/Onboarding started?	
Notes:		

Sagility	Avg. 30k-$60k	https://career.sagilityhealth.com/us/en
Yes/No	Job offered in your state and hiring?	
	What salary amount is offered?	
Yes/No	Do you like the opportunity, rate 1-5	
Yes/No	Resume/Cover letter sent/date	
Yes/No	Was the interview/Assessment Completed?	
Yes/No	Welcome Letter/Onboarding started?	
Notes:		

Saic	Avg. 44k-$60k	https://jobs.saic.com/
Yes/No	Job offered in your state and hiring?	
	What salary amount is offered?	
Yes/No	Do you like the opportunity, rate 1-5	
Yes/No	Resume/Cover letter sent/date	
Yes/No	Was the interview/Assessment Completed?	
Yes/No	Welcome Letter/Onboarding started?	
Notes:		

Sams Club	Avg. 30k-$50k	https://careers.walmart.com/stores-clubs/sams-club-jobs
Yes/No	Job offered in your state and hiring?	
	What salary amount is offered?	
Yes/No	Do you like the opportunity, rate 1-5	
Yes/No	Resume/Cover letter sent/date	
Yes/No	Was the interview/Assessment Completed?	
Yes/No	Welcome Letter/Onboarding started?	
Notes:		

Sedgwick	Avg. 30k-$50k	https://sedgwick.wd1.myworkdayjobs.com/en-US/Sedgwick?q=remote
Yes/No	Job offered in your state and hiring?	
	What salary amount is offered?	
Yes/No	Do you like the opportunity, rate 1-5	
Yes/No	Resume/Cover letter sent/date	
Yes/No	Was the interview/Assessment Completed?	
Yes/No	Welcome Letter/Onboarding started?	
Notes:		

Shutterfly	Avg. 41k-$50k	https://jobs.jobvite.com/shutterfly
Yes/No	Job offered in your state and hiring?	
	What salary amount is offered?	
Yes/No	Do you like the opportunity, rate 1-5	
Yes/No	Resume/Cover letter sent/date	
Yes/No	Was the interview/Assessment Completed?	
Yes/No	Welcome Letter/Onboarding started?	
Notes:		

Shift	Avg. 38k-$50k	https://shift.com/careers
Yes/No	Job offered in your state and hiring?	
	What salary amount is offered?	
Yes/No	Do you like the opportunity, rate 1-5	
Yes/No	Resume/Cover letter sent/date	
Yes/No	Was the interview/Assessment Completed?	
Yes/No	Welcome Letter/Onboarding started?	
Notes:		

Siemens Healthineers	Avg. 38k-$50k	https://www.siemens-healthineers.com/en-us/careers
Yes/No	Job offered in your state and hiring?	
	What salary amount is offered?	
Yes/No	Do you like the opportunity, rate 1-5	
Yes/No	Resume/Cover letter sent/date	
Yes/No	Was the interview/Assessment Completed?	
Yes/No	Welcome Letter/Onboarding started?	
Notes:		

Signet/Kay/ Jared Jewelers	Avg. 30k-$50k	https://www.signetjewelers.com/careers /
Yes/No	Job offered in your state and hiring?	
	What salary amount is offered?	
Yes/No	Do you like the opportunity, rate 1-5	
Yes/No	Resume/Cover letter sent/date	
Yes/No	Was the interview/Assessment Completed?	
Yes/No	Welcome Letter/Onboarding started?	
Notes:		

Sitel/ Foundever	Avg. 30k-$50k	https://jobs.foundever.com/go/Search-Jobs-US/
Yes/No	Job offered in your state and hiring?	
	What salary amount is offered?	
Yes/No	Do you like the opportunity, rate 1-5	
Yes/No	Resume/Cover letter sent/date	
Yes/No	Was the interview/Assessment Completed?	
Yes/No	Welcome Letter/Onboarding started?	
Notes:		

Slick Deals	Avg. 38k-$50k	https://slickdeals.net/corp/careers.html
Yes/No	Job offered in your state and hiring?	
	What salary amount is offered?	
Yes/No	Do you like the opportunity, rate 1-5	
Yes/No	Resume/Cover letter sent/date	
Yes/No	Was the interview/Assessment Completed?	
Yes/No	Welcome Letter/Onboarding started?	
Notes:		

Smith.Ai	Avg. 35k-$50k	https://smith.ai/careers
Yes/No	Job offered in your state and hiring?	
	What salary amount is offered?	
Yes/No	Do you like the opportunity, rate 1-5	
Yes/No	Resume/Cover letter sent/date	
Yes/No	Was the interview/Assessment Completed?	
Yes/No	Welcome Letter/Onboarding started?	
Notes:		

Softdocs	Avg. 40k-$50k	https://www.softdocs.com/company/careers
Yes/No	Job offered in your state and hiring?	
	What salary amount is offered?	
Yes/No	Do you like the opportunity, rate 1-5	
Yes/No	Resume/Cover letter sent/date	
Yes/No	Was the interview/Assessment Completed?	
Yes/No	Welcome Letter/Onboarding started?	
Notes:		

Southern Company	Avg. 43k-$150k	https://www.jobs.sutherlandglobal.com/ Home-office
Yes/No	Job offered in your state and hiring?	
	What salary amount is offered?	
Yes/No	Do you like the opportunity, rate 1-5	
Yes/No	Resume/Cover letter sent/date	
Yes/No	Was the interview/Assessment Completed?	
Yes/No	Welcome Letter/Onboarding started?	
Notes:		

Staples	Avg. 35k-$50k	https://careers.staples.com/global/en
Yes/No	Job offered in your state and hiring?	
	What salary amount is offered?	
Yes/No	Do you like the opportunity, rate 1-5	
Yes/No	Resume/Cover letter sent/date	
Yes/No	Was the interview/Assessment Completed?	
Yes/No	Welcome Letter/Onboarding started?	
Notes:		

State Farm	Avg. 33k-$50k	https://jobs.statefarm.com/main/
Yes/No	Job offered in your state and hiring?	
	What salary amount is offered?	
Yes/No	Do you like the opportunity, rate 1-5	
Yes/No	Resume/Cover letter sent/date	
Yes/No	Was the interview/Assessment Completed?	
Yes/No	Welcome Letter/Onboarding started?	
Notes:		

Sticker Mule	Avg. 43k-$50k	https://www.stickermule.com/careers
Yes/No	Job offered in your state and hiring?	
	What salary amount is offered?	
Yes/No	Do you like the opportunity, rate 1-5	
Yes/No	Resume/Cover letter sent/date	
Yes/No	Was the interview/Assessment Completed?	
Yes/No	Welcome Letter/Onboarding started?	
Notes:		

Sutherland	Avg. 33k-$50k	https://www.jobs.sutherlandglobal.com/
Yes/No	Job offered in your state and hiring?	
	What salary amount is offered?	
Yes/No	Do you like the opportunity, rate 1-5	
Yes/No	Resume/Cover letter sent/date	
Yes/No	Was the interview/Assessment Completed?	
Yes/No	Welcome Letter/Onboarding started?	
Notes:		

Sutter Health	Avg. 33k-$50k	https://www.sutterhealth.org/jobs
Yes/No	Job offered in your state and hiring?	
	What salary amount is offered?	
Yes/No	Do you like the opportunity, rate 1-5	
Yes/No	Resume/Cover letter sent/date	
Yes/No	Was the interview/Assessment Completed?	
Yes/No	Welcome Letter/Onboarding started?	
Notes:		

Sykes	Avg. 30k-$50k	https://sykesgroup.com/careers/
Yes/No	Job offered in your state and hiring?	
	What salary amount is offered?	
Yes/No	Do you like the opportunity, rate 1-5	
Yes/No	Resume/Cover letter sent/date	
Yes/No	Was the interview/Assessment Completed?	
Yes/No	Welcome Letter/Onboarding started?	
Notes:		

Synchrony	Avg. 30k-$50k	https://www.synchronycareers.com/
Yes/No	Job offered in your state and hiring?	
	What salary amount is offered?	
Yes/No	Do you like the opportunity, rate 1-5	
Yes/No	Resume/Cover letter sent/date	
Yes/No	Was the interview/Assessment Completed?	
Yes/No	Welcome Letter/Onboarding started?	
Notes:		

11 COMPANIES T-Z

Target	Avg. 30k-$50k	https://corporate.target.com/careers
Yes/No	Job offered in your state and hiring?	
	What salary amount is offered?	
Yes/No	Do you like the opportunity, rate 1-5	
Yes/No	Resume/Cover letter sent/date	
Yes/No	Was the interview/Assessment Completed?	
Yes/No	Welcome Letter/Onboarding started?	
Notes:		

Tele Performance	Avg. 30k-$50k	https://www.teleperformance.com/en-us/locations/usa-site/usa-careers
Yes/No	Job offered in your state and hiring?	
	What salary amount is offered?	
Yes/No	Do you like the opportunity, rate 1-5	
Yes/No	Resume/Cover letter sent/date	
Yes/No	Was the interview/Assessment Completed?	
Yes/No	Welcome Letter/Onboarding started?	
Notes:		

Telus International	Avg. 33k-$50k	https://www.telusinternational.com/careers
Yes/No	Job offered in your state and hiring?	
	What salary amount is offered?	
Yes/No	Do you like the opportunity, rate 1-5	
Yes/No	Resume/Cover letter sent/date	
Yes/No	Was the interview/Assessment Completed?	
Yes/No	Welcome Letter/Onboarding started?	
Notes:		

Tenet Health Care	Avg. 35k-$50k	https://jobs.tenethealth.com/
Yes/No	Job offered in your state and hiring?	
	What salary amount is offered?	
Yes/No	Do you like the opportunity, rate 1-5	
Yes/No	Resume/Cover letter sent/date	
Yes/No	Was the interview/Assessment Completed?	
Yes/No	Welcome Letter/Onboarding started?	
Notes:		

Thrivas	Avg. 38k-$50k	https://www.thrivas.com/jobs/
Yes/No	Job offered in your state and hiring?	
	What salary amount is offered?	
Yes/No	Do you like the opportunity, rate 1-5	
Yes/No	Resume/Cover letter sent/date	
Yes/No	Was the interview/Assessment Completed?	
Yes/No	Welcome Letter/Onboarding started?	
Notes:		

Thrivent	Avg. 38k-$50k	https://careers.thrivent.com/jobs/
Yes/No	Job offered in your state and hiring?	
	What salary amount is offered?	
Yes/No	Do you like the opportunity, rate 1-5	
Yes/No	Resume/Cover letter sent/date	
Yes/No	Was the interview/Assessment Completed?	
Yes/No	Welcome Letter/Onboarding started?	
Notes:		

Travel Pharmacy Bae	Avg. 80k-$150k	https://jobs.baesystems.com/global/en
Yes/No	Job offered in your state and hiring?	
	What salary amount is offered?	
Yes/No	Do you like the opportunity, rate 1-5	
Yes/No	Resume/Cover letter sent/date	
Yes/No	Was the interview/Assessment Completed?	
Yes/No	Welcome Letter/Onboarding started?	
Notes:		

Tria	Avg. 30k-$50k	https://triafed.com/careers/
Yes/No	Job offered in your state and hiring?	
	What salary amount is offered?	
Yes/No	Do you like the opportunity, rate 1-5	
Yes/No	Resume/Cover letter sent/date	
Yes/No	Was the interview/Assessment Completed?	
Yes/No	Welcome Letter/Onboarding started?	
Notes:		

Triad	Avg. 40k-$50k	https://triadincorporated.com/careers/
Yes/No	Job offered in your state and hiring?	
	What salary amount is offered?	
Yes/No	Do you like the opportunity, rate 1-5	
Yes/No	Resume/Cover letter sent/date	
Yes/No	Was the interview/Assessment Completed?	
Yes/No	Welcome Letter/Onboarding started?	
Notes:		

Triumpth Pay	Avg. 37k-$50k	https://apply.workable.com/triumphpay/
Yes/No	Job offered in your state and hiring?	
	What salary amount is offered?	
Yes/No	Do you like the opportunity, rate 1-5	
Yes/No	Resume/Cover letter sent/date	
Yes/No	Was the interview/Assessment Completed?	
Yes/No	Welcome Letter/Onboarding started?	
Notes:		

Trustmark Benefits	Avg. 32k-$50k	https://www.trustmarkbenefits.com/careers
Yes/No	Job offered in your state and hiring?	
	What salary amount is offered?	
Yes/No	Do you like the opportunity, rate 1-5	
Yes/No	Resume/Cover letter sent/date	
Yes/No	Was the interview/Assessment Completed?	
Yes/No	Welcome Letter/Onboarding started?	
Notes:		

Ttec	Avg. 30k-$50k	https://www.ttecjobs.com/
Yes/No	Job offered in your state and hiring?	
	What salary amount is offered?	
Yes/No	Do you like the opportunity, rate 1-5	
Yes/No	Resume/Cover letter sent/date	
Yes/No	Was the interview/Assessment Completed?	
Yes/No	Welcome Letter/Onboarding started?	
Notes:		

Uhaul	Avg. 30k-$50k	https://jobs.uhaul.com/	
Yes/No	Job offered in your state and hiring?		
	What salary amount is offered?		
Yes/No	Do you like the opportunity, rate 1-5		
Yes/No	Resume/Cover letter sent/date		
Yes/No	Was the interview/Assessment Completed?		
Yes/No	Welcome Letter/Onboarding started?		
Notes:			

Ultipro	Avg. 30k-$50k	https://www.indeed.com/	
Yes/No	Job offered in your state and hiring?		
	What salary amount is offered?		
Yes/No	Do you like the opportunity, rate 1-5		
Yes/No	Resume/Cover letter sent/date		
Yes/No	Was the interview/Assessment Completed?		
Yes/No	Welcome Letter/Onboarding started?		
Notes:			

United Health Care UHC	Avg. 33k-$50k	https://www.uhc.com/about-us/careers	
Yes/No	Job offered in your state and hiring?		
	What salary amount is offered?		
Yes/No	Do you like the opportunity, rate 1-5		
Yes/No	Resume/Cover letter sent/date		
Yes/No	Was the interview/Assessment Completed?		
Yes/No	Welcome Letter/Onboarding started?		
Notes:			

University of KY STEPS	Avg. 38k-$50k	https://www.indeed.com/
Yes/No	Job offered in your state and hiring?	
	What salary amount is offered?	
Yes/No	Do you like the opportunity, rate 1-5	
Yes/No	Resume/Cover letter sent/date	
Yes/No	Was the interview/Assessment Completed?	
Yes/No	Welcome Letter/Onboarding started?	
Notes:		

UOP.Avature.net	Avg. 50k-$70k	https://uop.avature.net/talentcommunity
Yes/No	Job offered in your state and hiring?	
	What salary amount is offered?	
Yes/No	Do you like the opportunity, rate 1-5	
Yes/No	Resume/Cover letter sent/date	
Yes/No	Was the interview/Assessment Completed?	
Yes/No	Welcome Letter/Onboarding started?	
Notes:		

US Acute Care	Avg. 32k-$50k	https://www.usacs.com/corporate-openings
Yes/No	Job offered in your state and hiring?	
	What salary amount is offered?	
Yes/No	Do you like the opportunity, rate 1-5	
Yes/No	Resume/Cover letter sent/date	
Yes/No	Was the interview/Assessment Completed?	
Yes/No	Welcome Letter/Onboarding started?	
Notes:		

US Bank	Avg. 32k-$50k	https://careers.usbank.com/global/en/
Yes/No	Job offered in your state and hiring?	
	What salary amount is offered?	
Yes/No	Do you like the opportunity, rate 1-5	
Yes/No	Resume/Cover letter sent/date	
Yes/No	Was the interview/Assessment Completed?	
Yes/No	Welcome Letter/Onboarding started?	
Notes:		

USA Jobs	Avg. 30k-$150k	https://www.usajobs.gov/
Yes/No	Job offered in your state and hiring?	
	What salary amount is offered?	
Yes/No	Do you like the opportunity, rate 1-5	
Yes/No	Resume/Cover letter sent/date	
Yes/No	Was the interview/Assessment Completed?	
Yes/No	Welcome Letter/Onboarding started?	
Notes:		

USAA	Avg. 42k-$100k	https://www.usaajobs.com/
Yes/No	Job offered in your state and hiring?	
	What salary amount is offered?	
Yes/No	Do you like the opportunity, rate 1-5	
Yes/No	Resume/Cover letter sent/date	
Yes/No	Was the interview/Assessment Completed?	
Yes/No	Welcome Letter/Onboarding started?	
Notes:		

Vacasa	Avg. 32k-$50k	https://www.vacasa.com/careers/positions
Yes/No	Job offered in your state and hiring?	
	What salary amount is offered?	
Yes/No	Do you like the opportunity, rate 1-5	
Yes/No	Resume/Cover letter sent/date	
Yes/No	Was the interview/Assessment Completed?	
Yes/No	Welcome Letter/Onboarding started?	
Notes:		

Walgreens	Avg. 30k-$150k	https://jobs.walgreens.com/en
Yes/No	Job offered in your state and hiring?	
	What salary amount is offered?	
Yes/No	Do you like the opportunity, rate 1-5	
Yes/No	Resume/Cover letter sent/date	
Yes/No	Was the interview/Assessment Completed?	
Yes/No	Welcome Letter/Onboarding started?	
Notes:		

Walmart	Avg. 30k-$50k	https://careers.walmart.com/
Yes/No	Job offered in your state and hiring?	
	What salary amount is offered?	
Yes/No	Do you like the opportunity, rate 1-5	
Yes/No	Resume/Cover letter sent/date	
Yes/No	Was the interview/Assessment Completed?	
Yes/No	Welcome Letter/Onboarding started?	
Notes:		

Wand, non violent felons	Avg. 30k-$50k	https://www.wand.org/careers
Yes/No	Job offered in your state and hiring?	
	What salary amount is offered?	
Yes/No	Do you like the opportunity, rate 1-5	
Yes/No	Resume/Cover letter sent/date	
Yes/No	Was the interview/Assessment Completed?	
Yes/No	Welcome Letter/Onboarding started?	
Notes:		

Wayfair	Avg. 30k-$50k	https://www.wayfair.com/careers/jobs
Yes/No	Job offered in your state and hiring?	
	What salary amount is offered?	
Yes/No	Do you like the opportunity, rate 1-5	
Yes/No	Resume/Cover letter sent/date	
Yes/No	Was the interview/Assessment Completed?	
Yes/No	Welcome Letter/Onboarding started?	
Notes:		

Weight Watchers	Avg. 30k-$50k	https://www.weightwatchers.com/us/ww-corporate-careers
Yes/No	Job offered in your state and hiring?	
	What salary amount is offered?	
Yes/No	Do you like the opportunity, rate 1-5	
Yes/No	Resume/Cover letter sent/date	
Yes/No	Was the interview/Assessment Completed?	
Yes/No	Welcome Letter/Onboarding started?	
Notes:		

Williams Lea	Avg. 32k-$50k	https://www.williamslea.com/careers
Yes/No	Job offered in your state and hiring?	
	What salary amount is offered?	
Yes/No	Do you like the opportunity, rate 1-5	
Yes/No	Resume/Cover letter sent/date	
Yes/No	Was the interview/Assessment Completed?	
Yes/No	Welcome Letter/Onboarding started?	
Notes:		

Williams Sonoma	Avg. 30k-$50k	https://www.williams-sonomainc.com/careers/jobs/
Yes/No	Job offered in your state and hiring?	
	What salary amount is offered?	
Yes/No	Do you like the opportunity, rate 1-5	
Yes/No	Resume/Cover letter sent/date	
Yes/No	Was the interview/Assessment Completed?	
Yes/No	Welcome Letter/Onboarding started?	
Notes:		

WM Dispatcher	Avg. 30k-$150k	https://www.wm.com/careers/
Yes/No	Job offered in your state and hiring?	
	What salary amount is offered?	
Yes/No	Do you like the opportunity, rate 1-5	
Yes/No	Resume/Cover letter sent/date	
Yes/No	Was the interview/Assessment Completed?	
Yes/No	Welcome Letter/Onboarding started?	
Notes:		

Work Bright	Avg. 34k-$50k	https://workbright.com/careers//
Yes/No	Job offered in your state and hiring?	
	What salary amount is offered?	
Yes/No	Do you like the opportunity, rate 1-5	
Yes/No	Resume/Cover letter sent/date	
Yes/No	Was the interview/Assessment Completed?	
Yes/No	Welcome Letter/Onboarding started?	
Notes:		

Working Solutions	Avg. 30k-$120k	https://jobs.workingsolutions.com/
Yes/No	Job offered in your state and hiring?	
	What salary amount is offered?	
Yes/No	Do you like the opportunity, rate 1-5	
Yes/No	Resume/Cover letter sent/date	
Yes/No	Was the interview/Assessment Completed?	
Yes/No	Welcome Letter/Onboarding started?	
Notes:		

WTW	Avg. 35k-$150k	https://careers.wtwco.com/
Yes/No	Job offered in your state and hiring?	
	What salary amount is offered?	
Yes/No	Do you like the opportunity, rate 1-5	
Yes/No	Resume/Cover letter sent/date	
Yes/No	Was the interview/Assessment Completed?	
Yes/No	Welcome Letter/Onboarding started?	
Notes:		

X Adecco USA	Avg. 30k-$150k	https://www.adeccousa.com/jobs/
Yes/No	Job offered in your state and hiring?	
	What salary amount is offered?	
Yes/No	Do you like the opportunity, rate 1-5	
Yes/No	Resume/Cover letter sent/date	
Yes/No	Was the interview/Assessment Completed?	
Yes/No	Welcome Letter/Onboarding started?	
Notes:		

XPO	Avg. 33k-$150k	https://jobs.xpo.com/
Yes/No	Job offered in your state and hiring?	
	What salary amount is offered?	
Yes/No	Do you like the opportunity, rate 1-5	
Yes/No	Resume/Cover letter sent/date	
Yes/No	Was the interview/Assessment Completed?	
Yes/No	Welcome Letter/Onboarding started?	
Notes:		

Zillow	Avg. 45k-$150k	https://www.zillow.com/careers/life-at-zillow/
Yes/No	Job offered in your state and hiring?	
	What salary amount is offered?	
Yes/No	Do you like the opportunity, rate 1-5	
Yes/No	Resume/Cover letter sent/date	
Yes/No	Was the interview/Assessment Completed?	
Yes/No	Welcome Letter/Onboarding started?	
Notes:		

12 DISCLOSURES

Disclosures

NEVER send any money for equipment, drug testing, background checks, or job offers. Please note, many scams duplicate real WFH positions from real, trusted corporations. If you are in doubt of a position please reach out to the company's career contact page to verify the position and apply on their website for a safer experience. Most reputable companies DO NOT use Telegram to interview.

The information and material contained in this document are solely for general information purposes and the Author cannot be held responsible for any decisions made based on it. Although we strive to keep the information accurate and up-to-date, we do not make any warranties or representations of any kind, express or implied, regarding the completeness, accuracy, reliability, suitability, or availability of the document or the information, products, services, or related graphics contained therein. Any reliance on such material is at your own risk. The Author will not be held liable for any false, inaccurate, inappropriate, or incomplete information presented on the website or services. Our role is to support and assist you in achieving your goals, but your success depends primarily on your own effort, motivation, commitment, and follow-through. We cannot guarantee any specific outcome or result, as each individual's results depend on various factors such as their unique background, dedication, desire, motivation, actions, and more. By using the information provided on this document or through our services, you fully agree that there are no guarantees as to the specific outcome or result you can expect.

I want to express my gratitude for joining me on this incredible journey and dedicating your precious time to reading my book. May fortune smile upon you as you pursue your dreams, and may you discover the same joy and fulfillment that I have found while working from the comfort of my own home. The freedom from commuting and the flexibility to be there for my children when they need me are just some of the reasons why I cherish this opportunity. Spending quality time with my children truly holds the utmost importance in my life.